MACHINE LEARNING FOR KIDS

A PROJECT-BASED INTRODUCTION TO ARTIFICIAL INTELLIGENCE

by Dale Lane

no starch press

MACHINE LEARNING FOR KIDS. Copyright © 2021 by Dale Lane.

Printed in the United States of America

First printing

24 23 22 21   1 2 3 4 5 6 7 8 9

ISBN-13: 978-1-7185-0056-3 (print)
ISBN-13: 978-1-7185-0057-0 (ebook)

Publisher: William Pollock
Executive Editor: Barbara Yien
Production Editor: Rachel Monaghan
Developmental Editors: Patrick DiJusto and Athabasca Witschi
Cover and Interior Design: Octopod Studios
Technical Reviewer: Maya Posch
Copyeditor: Rachel Monaghan
Compositor: Happenstance Type-O-Rama
Proofreader: Holly Bauer Forsyth

For information on book distributors or translations, please contact No Starch Press, Inc. directly:
No Starch Press, Inc.
245 8th Street, San Francisco, CA 94103
phone: 1-415-863-9900; info@nostarch.com
www.nostarch.com

Library of Congress Cataloging-in-Publication Data

Names: Lane, Dale, author.
Title: Machine learning for kids : a project-based introduction to
    artificial intelligence / Dale Lane.
Description: San Francisco : No Starch Press, [2020] | Includes index. |
    Summary: "An introduction to machine learning and artificial
    intelligence, using the Scratch programming language. Provides
    instructions to make a game that can learn hand motions, a chatbot that
    can answer questions, a computer assistant that can learn simple
    commands, and more"-- Provided by publisher.
Identifiers: LCCN 2020033935 (print) | LCCN 2020033936 (ebook) | ISBN
    9781718500563 (paperback) | ISBN 9781718500570 (ebook)
Subjects: LCSH: Artificial intelligence--Juvenile literature. | Machine
    learning--Juvenile literature. | Scratch (Computer program
    language)--Juvenile literature.
Classification: LCC Q335.4 .L36 2020 (print) | LCC Q335.4 (ebook) | DDC
    006.3/1--dc23
LC record available at https://lccn.loc.gov/2020033935
LC ebook record available at https://lccn.loc.gov/2020033936

ABOUT THE AUTHOR

Dale Lane is a senior developer for IBM with a background in artificial intelligence and machine learning. He has worked on a wide variety of AI projects for IBM clients and spent several years as a developer of IBM's AI platform Watson.

ABOUT THE TECHNICAL REVIEWER

Maya Posch is a software and hardware developer with a focus on C++, Ada, and VHDL. She works as a freelance developer in addition to writing fiction and nonfiction works.

CONTENTS IN BRIEF

CONTENTS IN DETAIL

12
AVOIDING THE MONSTER   185

13
TIC TAC TOE   203

14
CONFUSING THE COMPUTER   223

ACKNOWLEDGMENTS

I've had a huge amount of help to make this book happen, so I owe a lot of thanks to the staff at No Starch Press, including my publisher, Bill Pollock; my editor, Barbara Yien; my production editor and copyeditor, Rachel Monaghan; my developmental editors, Patrick DiJusto and Athabasca Witschi; and my technical reviewer, Maya Posch.

I am very grateful to the Lifelong Kindergarten Group at the MIT Media Lab for inventing Scratch, having the foresight to include a mechanism for extending it with new blocks, and generously making it all available (including the source code) free of charge. They make it possible for projects like Machine Learning for Kids to be built.

Finally, I'd like to thank John Keble CofE Primary School in Hursley for allowing me to develop and test the projects in this book with their students.

FOREWORD

When my dad was a child, growing up in Illinois after the turn of the century—not *this* century, mind you, but the *previous* one—radio was getting started, the zipper had just been invented, Charlie Chaplin was all the rage, Lindberg had not yet crossed the Atlantic, the *Titanic* sunk, the Model T was released, and most of the world was still being governed by various monarchies or vast, sprawling empires. When I was a child, growing up in the Great Plains of Texas, we had just landed humans on the moon, computers were huge, expensive beasts, the internet had not yet been invented, plastic was starting to become widespread, and talking to someone on the other side of the world was prohibitively expensive for all but a few. I spent many a lazy summer afternoon making gunpowder in my bedroom (sorry, Mom!), launching model rockets, and dreaming about going to the stars. I built my first computer from scratch when I was 12, and when I say "from scratch," I mean literally from individual transistors, diodes, resistors, and transistors. I'd read about this remarkable robot called Shakey by the good folks at the Stanford Research Institute, and I sat mesmerized in the movie theater watching HAL from *2001: A Space Odyssey*. I knew then and there that I wanted to build computers that would take people to the stars.

And now, here I am, doing very much that.

Right now, the world is a very, very different place than what my father and I experienced growing up. In some ways it's better, in others it is not, but one thing that has not changed is our ability to dream and to work to make those dreams become reality. Today, you can gain access to the world's knowledge using a device you can hold in your hand. It's possible to talk—and see—someone on the other side of the world, or even in space, in real time. Cars are now electric, and some of them even drive themselves. Not only have we gone to the moon, but Mars is now populated entirely by robots, and we have sent spacecraft beyond our solar system. Thanks to computers, we can produce more for less, we make art that augments and even transcends reality, we have extended our bodies and our minds, and we study the cosmos in ways far deeper and broader than we'd ever imagined.

The even more remarkable thing is that, owing to the fact that computers have gotten so inexpensive and their computational power so vast, almost anyone can learn how to use computers to build things that are limited only by our imagination. This is where *computational thinking* comes in, a way of approaching the world in terms of abstractions and algorithms that make it possible to turn our imagination into systems that run on our computers. To build a program that does your finances, or controls the heating in your house, or calculates the trajectory of a rocket flung into space, you'll think mostly in terms of symbols. But, if you want to build a car that drives itself, a robot that interacts safely with humans, or a video game that gives challenging virtual opponents, you'll need to use a different way of working with computers, and that is where artificial intelligence and machine learning come into play. From the time of Alan Turing—one of the pioneers of computing—computer scientists have tried to make computers that reason and learn and behave as humans, and recent advances in machine learning have made it possible for us today to build such things.

In this book, you'll learn the fundamentals of AI and ML, enough so that you'll build your own games and cognitive assistants, as well as programs that can discern language and images. As a child, my dad would have seen what you'll do here as utter magic, but as you'll discover, it's not really magic, it's just software, and mastering the computer to do all these things is well within your ability.

What delights me about this book is that it's wonderfully pragmatic, for it guides you in building AI systems that are very much relevant to contemporary computer science. Furthermore, the book doesn't shy away from the hard parts: along the way, you'll learn about biases and other ethical issues in using ML—issues that, as you progress in your work beyond this book, will become more and more important.

I wish I had a book like this when I was growing up. But then, such a book could not have existed, for most of the ideas presented here simply had not yet been invented. So, here's my challenge to you: after learning about AI and ML, what will you invent that no one has yet done?

—Grady Booch
IBM Fellow and Chief Scientist
for Software Engineering, IBM Research

INTRODUCTION

rtificial intelligence (AI) and machine learning (ML) systems impact all of us. Most of us use AI systems every day. They influence the news we read and hear; the decisions that companies and governments make; and what we choose to buy, watch, and listen to. They can even influence the jobs we get and where we live.

A great way to learn about AI technologies is to try making things that use them, and that's what this book will help you do. Building your own AI projects will help you to understand how these technologies behave and what they're capable of. It's also a fantastic introduction to the risks involved in using AI, as you'll see for yourself how things can go wrong.

Making your own projects based on how AI is used in the real world can also open your eyes to exactly how AI systems impact all of us. As you learn how everyday AI applications are created, you'll probably find that you start noticing AI systems and applications all around you. This gives you better insight into how the world around us works.

AI systems are often discussed on the news, but it can be difficult to think about what these stories mean if you don't have a basic understanding of the technologies involved. The projects in this book will prepare you to follow and engage in discussions of how AI systems are used, controlled, and regulated.

Finally, the projects in the book are meant to be fun! ML is a fascinating field of technology that makes it possible to create things that we couldn't otherwise. I hope you'll enjoy building something you didn't know how to build before and learning new techniques and tools in the process.

SCRATCH

Each chapter in this book introduces a new idea about the application or use of ML by walking you through a hands-on project in the educational coding platform *Scratch*. If you've used Scratch in school or in a coding club, you might already be familiar with it.

The Scratch projects in this book are all explained with detailed step-by-step instructions, so don't worry if you aren't an expert at using Scratch. However, if you've never used Scratch before, you might find it useful to visit the Scratch website to try it out (*https://scratch.mit.edu/*).

Before we get started, let's go over a few pointers and introduce the Scratch terminology that will be used throughout the book.

WORKING IN THE SCRATCH INTERFACE

The main sections of the Scratch interface are labeled in
Figure 1.

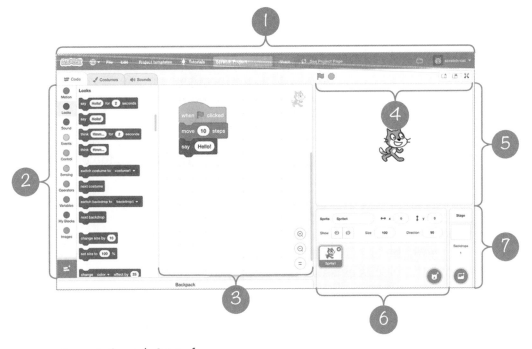

Figure 1: Scratch 3 interface

1. The *menu* contains the options for saving your project to or
   loading it from a file. It also includes a link to the Project
   templates library, which is a set of starter projects to help
   save you time.

2. The *Toolbox* is a palette of blocks available for you to use in
   your program.

3. The *Code Area* is where you create your programs when
   the Code tab is active. Drag blocks from the Toolbox
   onto the Code Area to create your projects. When the
   Backdrops or Costumes tab is active, this area contains
   drawing and painting tools and is known as the *canvas*.

4. The *controls* allow you to run your program when you want to try it out. The Green Flag starts your code running, and the Stop Sign stops it. The rightmost button with four arrows runs your program in full-screen mode.

5. The *Stage* is where you prepare the visual part of your program. You'll move the different components of your project around in here.

6. *Sprites* are the objects that perform the actions in your project. Each sprite has its own look (called a *costume*) and will have its own code in the Code Area.

7. *Backdrops* are the backgrounds for your project. You can draw your own or choose from a library of premade options.

CODING IN SCRATCH

You create your program—known as a *script* in Scratch—by dragging blocks from the Toolbox to the Code Area. When you move the blocks close to each other, they snap together.

MATCHING COLORS

Scratch blocks are color coded by category. For example, *Motion blocks*, the blocks you use to move your sprite, are blue. To access them, you click the blue circle labeled Motion in the Toolbox.

When you're copying code for this book's projects, this color coding will help you find the blocks you need more easily. If the project requires a yellow block, click the yellow Events circle to go directly to the Events blocks in the Toolbox and select the one you need.

CREATING CUSTOM BLOCKS

Pink blocks are custom blocks. They let you split up a long code script into smaller pieces to make it easier to read.

To create a custom block, click **Make a Block** in the My Blocks section of the Toolbox as shown in Figure 2.

Give your new custom block a name and then click **OK**. This will create a new pink custom block that you can use in the same way as any other Scratch block.

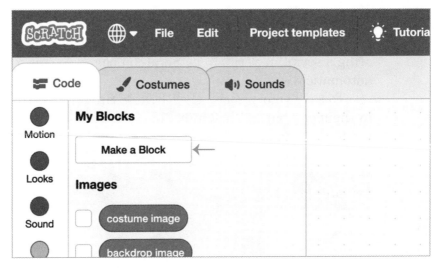

Figure 2: Click **Make a Block** to create your own custom blocks.

Put the script with the steps you want your custom block to carry out under the big pink **define** block, as shown in Figure 3.

Figure 3: Custom blocks are available in the Toolbox and can be used like any other Scratch block.

DUPLICATING

If you're creating a long code script with similar sections, you can *duplicate* those sections to save yourself time.

Right-click the section of the code you want to copy and choose **duplicate**. This tip will be very useful for several of the projects in this book.

SAVING YOUR WORK

It's important to save your work regularly when you're creating a script in Scratch, as Scratch doesn't do this for you automatically.

To save your project, click **File ▶ Save to your computer** in the menu bar as shown in Figure 4. This will download a file to the computer. Keep this file safe—it's your copy of the project you've created.

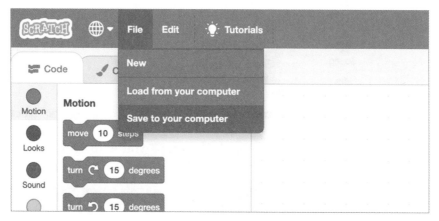

Figure 4: The File menu in Scratch lets you save your projects to work on later.

To open this project again, click **File ▶ Load from your computer** and choose the file you've saved.

MACHINE LEARNING FOR KIDS

The projects in this book use *Machine Learning for Kids*, a free online tool that extends Scratch to add the ML capabilities you'll be using. Don't worry if you haven't used this tool before. Chapter 2 will cover everything you need to know to get started with it.

WHAT'S NEXT?

The book is organized as follows:

Chapter 1, What Is Artificial Intelligence?
You'll learn more about AI and ML, and why we use ML instead of traditional programming for our projects.

Chapter 2, Introducing Machine Learning for Kids

Here you'll learn all about the tool you'll be using in the rest of the book to build your own ML projects.

The rest of the book covers different things that ML systems can be trained to recognize.

Chapter 3, Sorting Animal Pictures

In this chapter, you'll learn about image recognition. You'll train the computer to recognize objects in a photo and then have it automatically sort pictures of animals.

Chapter 4, Playing Rock, Paper, Scissors Against Your Computer

In this project, you'll use a webcam to train an ML system to recognize different hand shapes so you can play Rock, Paper, Scissors against your computer!

Chapter 5, Recognizing Movie Posters

You'll learn how computers can be trained to recognize artistic styles, not just objects, in pictures. After training a computer to judge a book by its cover, you'll find out whether computers can learn to be creative.

Chapter 6, Mail Sorting

This chapter explains how computers can learn to recognize writing. Then you'll build a simple system that uses handwriting recognition to sort envelopes.

Chapter 7, Insulting a Computer

In this chapter, you'll learn how computers can be trained to recognize tone in writing. You'll train a computer game character to recognize and react to your compliments and insults.

Chapter 8, Recognizing Language in Newspapers

Here you'll train a computer to recognize different styles of writing to predict which newspaper an article probably came from. We'll also discuss ways of measuring how good an ML system is.

Chapter 9, Finding an Object in a Picture

This chapter builds on earlier projects and covers how to train a computer to find a smaller object in a picture. We'll talk about some of the ways that this technique is used in real-world applications like processing satellite images and training self-driving cars.

Chapter 10, Smart Assistants

In this chapter, you'll see how computers can be trained to recognize the meaning of text, and how this technology is used to program smart assistants. You'll make a simple assistant that can understand your commands to turn different things on and off.

Chapter 11, Chatbots

Here you'll learn about chatbots, and how computers that are able to recognize the meaning of text can be used to build question answering systems.

Chapter 12, Avoiding the Monster

This chapter explains how computer games have been used to develop AI technologies. You'll train an ML system to play a simplified version of *Pac-Man*.

Chapter 13, Tic Tac Toe

Here you'll see another example of computer games and AI, by re-creating a version of a famous AI research project to train a computer to play Tic Tac Toe.

Chapter 14, Confusing the Computer

You'll see firsthand how ML projects most commonly go wrong, by creating your own confused AI system that makes mistakes. You'll learn about the problems this causes, and steps we can take to avoid it.

Chapter 15, Biasing the Computer

In this chapter, you'll learn about how some people intentionally influence the answers that their ML projects give and some of the AI ethics issues this raises.

Afterword

The book ends with a look ahead to what the future of AI might hold.

1
WHAT IS ARTIFICIAL INTELLIGENCE?

n this book, we'll be exploring different aspects of AI by building projects based on real-world uses of ML. Before we get started, though, it will be useful to go over some background information on the tools and technologies we'll be working with.

In the introduction, you met the Scratch programming language and learned what each section of the Scratch interface does. This chapter will explain a few basic programming terms and concepts that we'll use in the rest of the book.

CODING

Coding is how we tell machines what we want them to do. We often use code to control computers, but we also use it to control small devices like mobile phones, household appliances like washing machines, and huge machines like cars and airplanes.

To write code, we first have to understand the task that we want the machine to do, and then we break that task down into a series of steps. The steps need to be specific and detailed enough for the machine to follow.

Some programming languages, like Scratch, try to explain coding with colored blocks that represent those steps. You snap blocks together to describe the sequence of steps the machine should take, as shown in Figure 1-1.

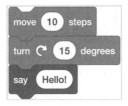

Figure 1-1: Scratch explains coding using
colored blocks that snap together.

Describing tasks as a series of steps for a machine to follow has been the job of *software developers* for decades. We have more expressive programming languages now that make it easier to describe steps than it was in the past, but the basic idea is still the same.

However, while coding is useful, these days our machines are so complicated that it's no longer enough. For example, a new car has over 100 million lines of code to accomplish all of its different tasks. That's like having to write 100 million steps!

Some tasks that we want machines to do are so complicated that it would take way too long to write step-by-step instructions for them—and sometimes we don't even know how to describe the steps.

For these sorts of tasks, we use ML.

MACHINE LEARNING

ML is useful for tasks with steps that would take too long to write or that are too complex to describe. Instead of describing a task's exact steps to a machine, we can use ML to show the machine examples of the task over and over again until it learns how to perform that task.

Imagine getting someone to kick a ball. You could give them exact step-by-step instructions: how high to lift their leg, how fast to move their leg, what to do with their arms, and so on. Giving them step-by-step instructions is the coding approach.

Instead, you could show the person lots of examples of people kicking different kinds of balls and let them learn that way. Collecting and showing examples of the task to perform—known as *training*—is the ML approach.

Throughout this book, you'll see lots of examples of how ML systems are trained, how they behave, and how they are used.

ARTIFICIAL INTELLIGENCE

People sometimes confuse ML with AI. Some of the most interesting AI systems have been built using ML, but it isn't the only way to build an AI system. The relationship between the two is illustrated in Figure 1-2.

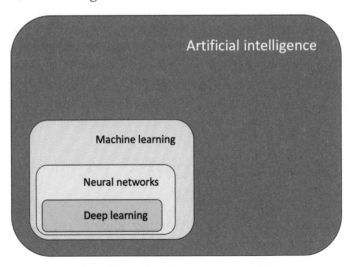

Figure 1-2: The relationship between ML and AI

Artificial intelligence is a general term used to describe projects where a machine is doing something that would normally require human intelligence. It doesn't say anything about *how* you get the machine to do that thing, and there are lots of different techniques you can use. ML is just one way to make an AI project (just like neural networks, which we'll discuss shortly, are just one kind of ML). Let's look at an example to better understand the difference.

In 1997, a computer called Deep Blue beat the world champion Garry Kasparov at a game of chess. Deep Blue was an AI project, and many described it as a landmark in AI development.

But it wasn't an ML system. Deep Blue didn't learn how to play chess or how to win; it was programmed. People coded the system with the rules of the game, and more importantly, the strategies for winning. The computer just followed the instructions that it was given, step by step.

That was still enough to win. Deep Blue wasn't smarter than Kasparov, but it could follow more instructions and test out more possible moves quicker than he could.

In 2011, a computer called Watson beat *Jeopardy!* champions Ken Jennings and Brad Rutter at the US television quiz show. Watson, also an AI project, demonstrated the potential for future computer systems to learn and understand the way that humans use language.

Unlike Deep Blue, Watson was an ML system. It learned how to play the game show by being trained with the questions from every *Jeopardy!* episode going back to the 1960s, as well as by playing lots of practice matches against human competitors.

People still build AI systems like Deep Blue today, because simple AI systems that follow step-by-step instructions written by people can still be useful. However, ML can be used to build AI systems that do more complex and sophisticated jobs.

NEURAL NETWORKS AND DEEP LEARNING

Neural networks and deep learning, shown in Figure 1-2, are two types of ML. You won't learn about them in detail in this book, but since they're often mentioned in articles about AI, let's talk about how they relate to AI.

Neural networks are a popular and very powerful technique for building ML systems. They have proven effective at some very complex problems. Their structure is loosely based on the structure of animal brains, with the different parts of the ML system, called *neurons*, arranged in layers that are connected together.

Deep learning is a method for working with a neural network with a large number of layers, and it's one of the most effective techniques for building AI systems today.

Rather than describing specific ML approaches like these, this book will focus on ML in general. You'll learn about how ML systems typically behave, how they are trained and what issues can arise, and how they are used in the real world. After reading this book, you'll have the foundation you need to explore more specific applications of ML like neural networks and deep learning if you're interested in doing so.

WHAT YOU LEARNED

ML means training a computer to do a task by collecting examples of that task being performed. It is a popular way of building AI projects because it enables us to train the computer on more complicated tasks than we could describe with written step-by-step instructions.

2
INTRODUCING MACHINE LEARNING FOR KIDS

n this book, you'll be building ML projects using a free educational tool called Machine Learning for Kids. This chapter will introduce how the tool works, how you'll use it for each project, and how your parent or teacher can set it up for you.

You can find Machine Learning for Kids at *https://MachineLearningForKids.co.uk/*. It's a long web address to type, so it's a good idea to save a bookmark the first time you visit.

The home page is shown in Figure 2-1. (As with all websites, the design will change slightly over time, so it might look a little different than what's shown here.)

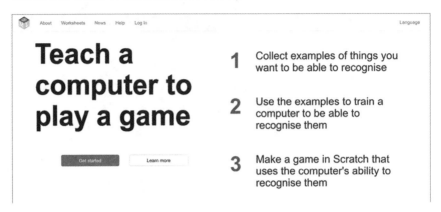

Figure 2-1: Machine Learning for Kids home page

LOGGING IN

The first step for every project in this book is to go to the Machine Learning for Kids site and log in.

Click **Log In** in the top menu bar. You'll see the login screen shown in Figure 2-2.

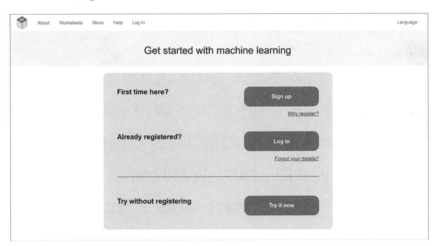

Figure 2-2: Machine Learning for Kids login page

You have two choices here:

Log in   If your parent or teacher has already created a free account for you, click **Log in** and enter your username and password. Logging in allows you to save your projects and come back to them later.

Try it now   If you don't have an account yet, click **Try it now**. You'll still be able to work on a project, but only for four hours. That's long enough to complete any of the projects in this book, but you won't be able to come back to them later.

The Sign up button, where your parent or teacher creates a free account for you, is explained in "Creating an Account" on page 14.

CREATING A NEW ML PROJECT

Once you've logged in, you'll be taken to a list of your projects, shown in Figure 2-3. You can get back to this list at any time by clicking Projects in the top menu bar.

Figure 2-3: An empty projects list

To create a new project, follow these steps:

1. Click **Add a new project** (see Figure 2-3).
2. Type a name for your project in the Project Name text box, shown in Figure 2-4.

   Each chapter in the book will suggest a name for the project, but you can enter a different name here if you prefer.

Figure 2-4: Creating a new ML project

3. Click **Recognising**, shown in Figure 2-4. You should see a drop-down list of different types of ML projects (Figure 2-5). This is where you select the category (for example, text or images) you want to teach the computer to recognize. Each project in the book will tell you which option to choose here.

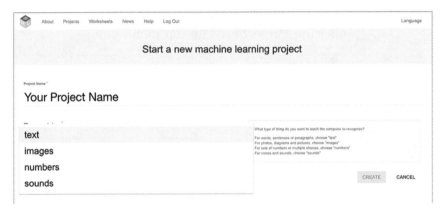

Figure 2-5: Choosing the type of ML project

4. Click **Create**.

5. You'll be taken back to your projects list, as shown in Figure 2-6. Click the name of the project you've just created to get started.

Figure 2-6: Updated projects list

PHASES OF AN ML PROJECT

There are three main phases to each project: Train, Learn & Test, and Make (see Figure 2-7).

You can switch to each phase by clicking its blue button. The project instructions will tell you when it's time to move on to each phase.

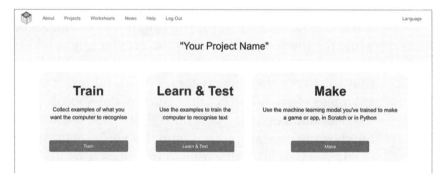

Figure 2-7: Phases of an ML project

TRAIN

In the Train phase, you collect examples of what you want the computer to learn to recognize.

You'll create a bucket for each subcategory you're training the computer to recognize. Each bucket has a gray border, as shown in Figure 2-8.

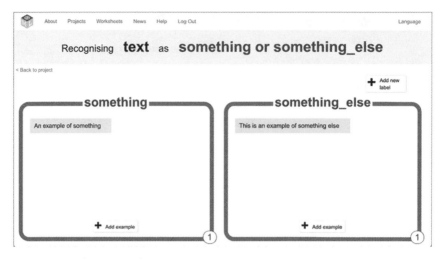

Figure 2-8: The Train phase

Next, you'll fill those buckets with examples. For text projects, that means collecting examples of writing that fall into each subcategory. In Figure 2-8, the buckets include text examples of the subcategories *something* and *something_else*. (In a real project, for the text subcategory *kind*, you might add examples of compliments, while for the text subcategory *mean*, you might add insults.) For image projects, you'll fill the buckets with examples of pictures that illustrate the subcategory. For sound projects, you'll collect examples of sound recordings that fit the subcategory.

The number at the bottom right of each bucket is a handy counter showing you how many examples you've collected so far.

If you've added an example to a bucket by accident and want to get rid of it, move your mouse pointer over it and click the red X.

If you want to remove an entire bucket, including all of its training examples, move your mouse pointer over the top-right corner of the bucket and click the red X. Be sure about this, because there's no way to get a bucket back once you've deleted it!

LEARN & TEST

Once you've collected enough examples, you're ready to use them to train an ML *model*. (The next chapter explains more about models.)

To start the training process, click **Train new machine learning model** (see Figure 2-9).

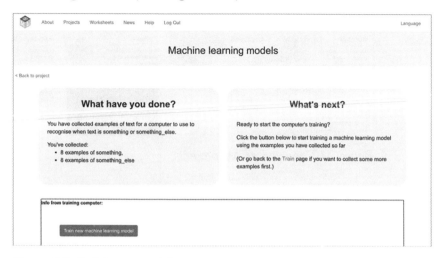

Figure 2-9: Training a model

How long this process takes depends on the type of project and the number of examples you've collected. Image projects take longer than text projects (because it's much harder for computers to understand images than to understand text or numbers). The more examples you have, the longer training will take. And sometimes the ML computer server will be busy and take a little longer.

The training process might take 30 seconds, or it might take a few minutes. Please be patient! There's a quiz at the bottom of the page to try while you wait.

If you haven't collected enough examples, you won't see the Train new machine learning model button. Go back to the Train phase to add more examples.

MAKE

Once you have an ML model, you can make something with it.

There are different types of projects that you can build, but all of the projects in this book use Scratch 3. Click **Scratch 3** as shown in Figure 2-10.

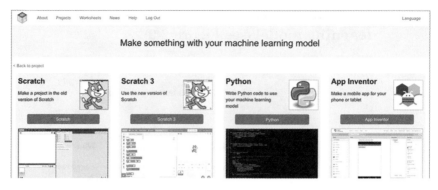

Figure 2-10: Making an ML project

Now you're ready to get started with the projects in this book! But remember, if you want to use the Log in option (instead of Try it now) so that you can save your projects, you'll need to ask an adult to create an account for you. Let's go over that now.

CREATING AN ACCOUNT

Creating an account is free and only has to be done once. There are 10 steps, and signing up can take up to 10 minutes. This section covers the instructions your parent, teacher, or coding club leader needs to follow.

NOTE *The adult creating the account will need to provide an email address. For information about how the email address will be used, they can go to* https://machinelearningforkids.co.uk/help/.

1. Click **Sign up** (shown in Figure 2-2).
2. Click the button confirming that you are a parent, teacher, or coding club leader.
3. Click **Sign up** under "Create an unmanaged class account." This means that you will be in charge of your account and are setting it up yourself.
4. Fill in the form shown in Figure 2-11. Choose a username and enter an email address where you can be contacted. You can optionally also describe how you're planning to use the site.

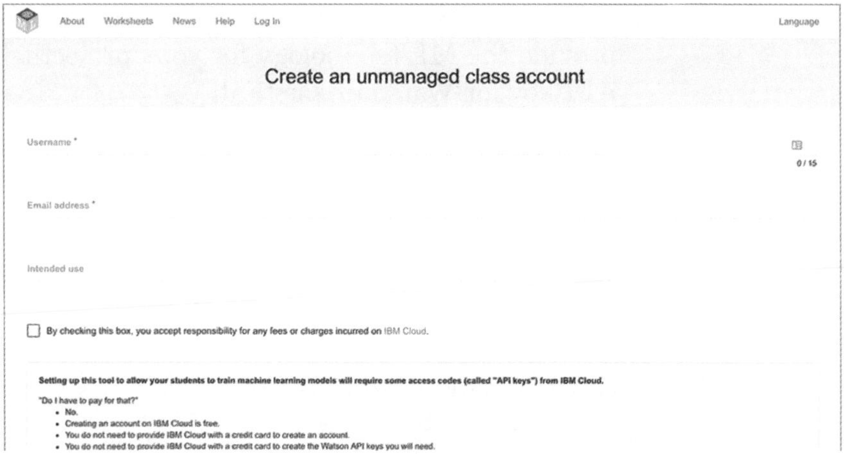

Figure 2-11: Creating a parent/teacher account

5. You'll be sent an email to verify your email address. Click the link in that email before continuing to the next step.

6. Once you log in with your parent/teacher account, you'll have access to the Administration page shown in Figure 2-12. Click **Teacher** in the top menu bar to go to the Administration page.

Figure 2-12: Parent/teacher screen

7. Click **Restrictions** to review the default restrictions for your account. Some of them can be altered to your preferences.

8. Click **API Keys** to enter the codes from IBM Cloud that will provide the ML technology for your projects. You'll need one API key for Watson Assistant.

    To create these codes, you'll need to create a free account on IBM Cloud. There is no charge for the Watson Assistant key codes.

    The IBM Cloud site can be a little daunting if you're not used to websites aimed at software developers. The step-by-step guide at *https://machinelearningforkids.co.uk/apikeys-guide/* explains exactly what to do.

NOTE   *Make sure to create* Lite *API keys. These are the free ones. They're limited in how much they can be used, but they're sufficient for building all of the projects in this book.*

9. Click **Students** to create a username for the student who will be doing the projects in this book. If multiple students will be building these projects, you can create multiple usernames.

    There's no need to use real names or provide any contact information for students.

    User accounts for students are simpler than those for teachers. Students don't have to worry about API keys from IBM or any other technical details.

    If they forget their password, you can reset it for them from the Students page.

10. Click **Supervision** to see a list of projects that students have created.

    It's unlikely that you'll hit the limit for the API keys you've added unless many students are working through the book at the same time. If that happens, you'll be able to see which projects are using the API keys here.

WHAT YOU LEARNED

Machine Learning for Kids is the free tool you'll be using for the projects in this book. The tool guides you through the main phases of an ML project. The project instructions will tell you exactly what to do at each phase and when you should move on to the next phase or return to a previous one.

If you want to be able to save your projects, you'll need an adult to create an account for you. Creating an account is a little complicated and can take 10 minutes or so, but the process is free, only has to be done once, and is explained in detail online.

3

SORTING ANIMAL PICTURES

We all love pictures. We take over a trillion digital photos every year, and that doesn't even include other types of pictures that we make, like drawings and paintings.

Using computers to sort pictures and help us find the ones we need is called *image recognition*. To create an image recognition system, we collect lots of pictures of the same subject. Then we use those pictures to train an ML *model*, which identifies what those pictures have in common and uses that to recognize new pictures.

For example, if we want to train a computer to recognize photos of kittens, we collect lots of photos of kittens. ML systems use these photos to learn the shapes, patterns, and colors that often show up in kitten photos. The model can then recognize whether a photo has a kitten in it.

People use image recognition every day. Online photo-sharing tools use it to help sort the photos that we upload. Websites use it to describe the contents of photos to help people with visual disabilities know what's in photos even if they can't see them. Social media websites use it to recognize the faces of our friends and family in the photos we post. Companies use it to track when their logos or products are included in photos posted online so they know when they're being talked about on social media. More importantly, doctors use it to help them recognize medical conditions in patients' scans and photos. Doctors need to remember many different symptoms and signs of illness, so image recognition systems can help them by identifying things like skin tumors in photographs or cancer in a microscopic picture of a cell.

In this chapter, you'll make your own image recognition system by training an ML model to recognize and automatically sort photos of animals. Let's get started!

BUILD YOUR PROJECT

First, choose two types of animals that you want the computer to recognize. For this chapter, I chose cows and sheep to make a farm-themed Scratch project (see Figure 3-1). You can choose any two animals you'd like, as long as you can easily find lots of photos of them.

Figure 3-1: Sorting photos of animals into groups

TRAIN YOUR MODEL

To train the computer to recognize different pictures of your two animals, you'll need to collect lots of images of those animals and use them to train an ML model.

1. Create a new ML project, enter **Animal sorter** as its name, and set it to learn to recognize images.

NOTE *If you're not sure how to create an ML project, read the section "Creating a New ML Project" on page 9 in Chapter 2.*

2. Click **Train**, as shown in Figure 3-2.

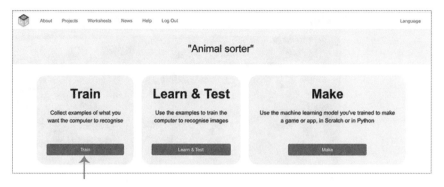

Figure 3-2: Train is the first phase of an ML project.

3. Click **Add new label** (see Figure 3-3). Then enter the name of your first type of animal.

Figure 3-3: Click **Add new label** *to create a new bucket of training examples.*

4. Open a second window in your web browser (usually by selecting **File ▶ New Window**) and arrange your two windows side by side, as shown in Figure 3-4. In the second window, search for photos of the first type of animal. In my case, I've searched for photos of cows.

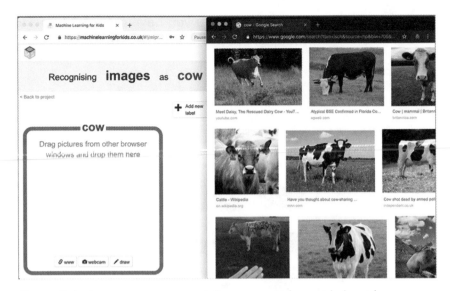

Figure 3-4: Arrange your two web browser windows side by side.

5. Drag a photo from the search window and drop it into the training bucket for your first type of animal. You should see a thumbnail version of the photo in your training bucket, as shown in Figure 3-5. If you don't see it, try dragging and dropping the photo again.

Figure 3-5: Dropping photos of cows into my training bucket

6. Repeat step 5 until you have at least 10 different photos of that animal, as shown in Figure 3-6.

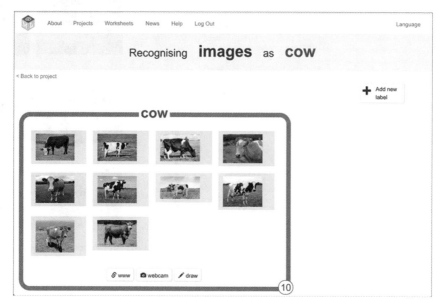

Figure 3-6: My training data for recognizing photos of cows

7. Repeat steps 3 through 6 until you have at least 10 different photos for each type of animal, as shown in Figure 3-7.

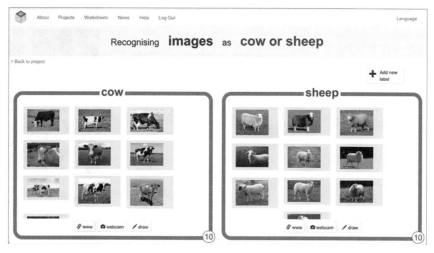

Figure 3-7: Training data for my farm-themed project

8. Click **Back to project** in the top-left corner of the screen.

9. Click **Learn & Test** (see Figure 3-8).

Figure 3-8: Learn & Test is the second phase of an ML project.

10. Click **Train new machine learning model** (see Figure 3-9).

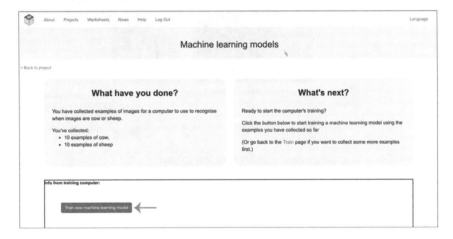

Figure 3-9: Click **Train new machine learning model** to start the training.

The computer will use the examples you've collected to learn what the photos of each animal have in common. This can take a few minutes, but you can continue to the next step in your second web browser window while you wait.

PREPARE YOUR PROJECT

To test your ML model, you'll need some new photos that you haven't used for training. The computer will use what it learns from your training examples to try to recognize your two animals in these new photos. Then you'll build a project in Scratch that tests how well your model performs.

1. Search for more photos of the animals you've chosen, and save them to your computer. To save a photo, right-click it and select **Save Picture** or **Save Image As**, as shown in Figure 3-10.

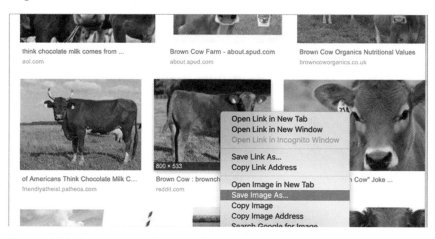

Figure 3-10: Saving test photos to the computer

NOTE

Don't choose the same photos you used for training the model. You want to test how good the computer is at recognizing new photos, not how good it is at remembering them.

2. Aim for at least five test photos of each type of animal that you chose, as shown in Figure 3-11.

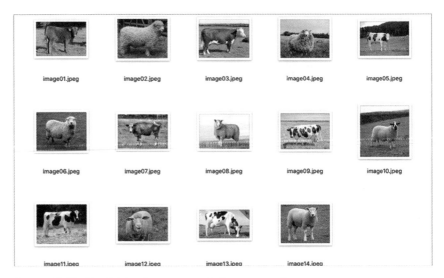

image01.jpeg	image02.jpeg	image03.jpeg	image04.jpeg	image05.jpeg
image06.jpeg	image07.jpeg	image08.jpeg	image09.jpeg	image10.jpeg
image11.jpeg	image12.jpeg	image13.jpeg	image14.jpeg	

Figure 3-11: My folder for cow and sheep test photos

3. Click **Back to project** in the top-left corner of the screen.

4. Click **Make** (see Figure 3-12).

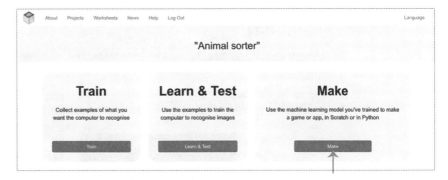

Figure 3-12: Make is the third phase of an ML project.

5. Click **Scratch 3**, and then click **Open in Scratch 3** to open a new window with Scratch.

You should see new blocks representing your ML model in the Toolbox, as shown in Figure 3-13.

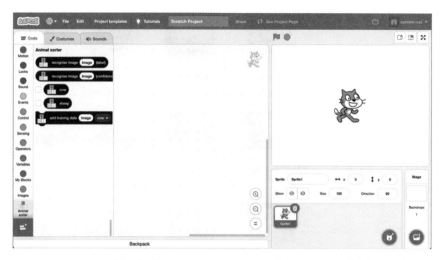

Figure 3-13: New blocks for your ML project will automatically be added to the Scratch Toolbox.

6. Create a backdrop for your project.

    In the bottom-right corner of the Scratch window, move your mouse pointer over the Choose a Backdrop icon, shown in Figure 3-14.

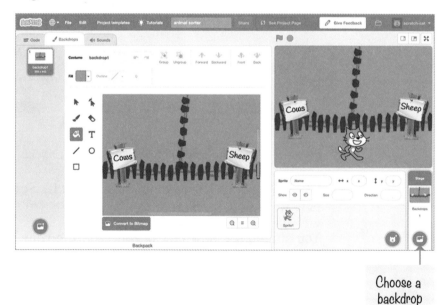

Choose a backdrop

Figure 3-14: My farm background for sorting cows and sheep into two groups

You have a few options here. If you don't like drawing, you can click **Choose a Backdrop** to pick a default background, or click **Upload Backdrop** to use a picture from the internet. To design your own background for your animals, click **Paint** and use the drawing and coloring tools in the *paint editor* to the left of the Code canvas.

No matter which option you choose, be sure to add clearly labeled sections to your backdrop for each type of animal.

I chose farm animals, so I drew a farm scene with signs labeled Cows and Sheep. You can draw something that fits with the animals you chose. For example, if you chose dogs and cats, you could draw a pet shop. If you chose lions and elephants, you could draw a zoo.

7. Click the cat sprite, and then in the bottom-left corner of the screen, move your mouse pointer over the Choose a Costume icon. Click **Upload Costume**, as shown in Figure 3-15.

8. Select all of the test photos you saved in step 2 to upload all of them at once.

NOTE   *Make sure you're doing this for the sprite, not the backdrop.*

Figure 3-15: Click **Upload Costume** to add your test photos. You can delete the cat costumes from the costume pane on the left.

9. If you missed any of your test photos, click **Upload Costume** again and repeat until you've uploaded all of the test photos from step 2.

We won't need the Scratch cat costumes, so you can delete them. In the *costume pane* on the far left (see Figure 3-15), click the costume and then click the trash can in its top-right corner to delete it.

Make sure that you upload costumes for the same single sprite, as shown in Figure 3-16. Don't upload each photo as a new sprite.

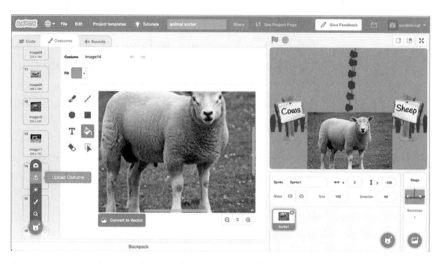

Figure 3-16: Upload additional costumes to the same sprite.

10. Click the **Code** tab and copy the scripts shown in Figure 3-17.

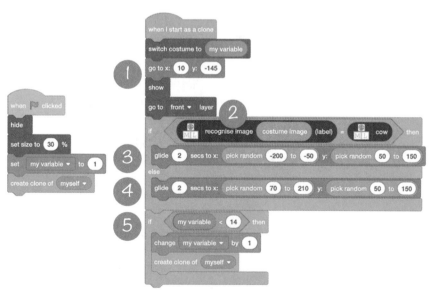

Figure 3-17: Example code for sorting photos of animals

If you're not sure how to code in Scratch, read "Coding in Scratch" on "Coding in Scratch" on page xxii in the introduction to this book.

This code will go through each of your test photo costumes and use your ML model to recognize the animal and move it to the correct section.

The go to x: 10 y: -145 block ❶ sets the starting position for each photo. This script will start each photo at the bottom middle of the screen. Adjust these coordinates to a starting position that fits with your backdrop.

The recognise image block ❷ uses your ML model to recognize the photo.

The glide to x: pick random -200 to -50 y: pick random 50 to 150 block ❸ moves the photo to a random position in the top left of the screen. Adjust these coordinates to the location on your backdrop where you want the photos of your first type of animal to go.

The glide to x: pick random 70 to 210 y: pick random 50 to 150 block ❹ moves the photo to a random position in the top right of the screen. Adjust these coordinates to the location on your backdrop where you want the photos of your second type of animal to go.

The number in if my variable is < 14 ❺ refers to how many test photos you have. Set this value to the number of test costumes you saved in step 2 and uploaded in step 8. I have 14 costumes in my test sprite, so my script goes through 14 test photos.

TEST YOUR MODEL

To test the model you've created, click the Green Flag in the top-left corner, as shown in Figure 3-18. Your model will sort your test photos into two groups of animals.

Count how many photos your model moves to the correct side. That's a simple way to measure how good your project is at sorting photos of your two animals.

Figure 3-18: Recognizing photos and sorting them into groups

If your model is getting a lot wrong, you can try to improve it using more training examples. Go back to the Train phase and drag in more photos of each of your animals. Then go back to the Learn & Test phase and train the new, improved ML model. Run your Scratch script again to see if the new model sorts more of your test photos correctly.

REVIEW AND IMPROVE YOUR PROJECT

You've successfully trained an ML model to recognize photos of animals! This project isn't based on rules. You haven't described how different animals look or given the computer specific instructions on how to recognize them. Instead, you've used ML to train the computer to do it. This approach is known as *supervised learning* because you supervised the process by preparing sets of training examples for the computer to use.

As long as your test photos are similar to your training photos, your model should work. However, if you test your model with pictures that differ somehow from your training photos, you'll probably get different results.

For example, I tried replacing the costumes in my Scratch project with cartoon illustrations of cows and sheep instead of photographs. Then I ran my code again by clicking the Green Flag. As you can see in Figure 3-19, my new model got a lot wrong.

Figure 3-19: ML models get a lot wrong if the test inputs aren't similar to the training inputs.

I got these results because the patterns my model learned to recognize from the training photos weren't useful to help it recognize cartoon drawings. If you want a computer to be able to recognize photographs *and* cartoons, you need to train it with both.

Go back to the Train phase and create a new set of training examples that includes both photographs and cartoons, as shown in Figure 3-20. I collected 10 example photos and 10 example cartoons in each bucket.

Figure 3-20: Training a computer to recognize both photos and cartoons

Then go back to the Learn & Test phase and train a new ML model using your new set of training examples. This new set should teach the computer to identify patterns in photographs and cartoons so it can recognize both. Figure 3-21 shows how much better my updated ML model performed.

Figure 3-21: Testing with a mixture of photographs and drawings

As you can see, the more similar the test images are to the training images that the computer learns from, the better ML models perform.

What other changes could you make to improve your model?

WHAT YOU LEARNED

In this chapter, you used ML to create an image recognition system capable of recognizing and sorting pictures of animals. You learned some of the key principles in ML projects, such as improving your results by increasing the number of training images and making sure they're similar to the images you want the computer to recognize.

You also learned that we can measure how well an image recognition system performs by trying it out with test pictures and counting how many it identifies correctly. You tried this yourself by creating a project in Scratch to test how well your ML model sorted a group of animal photos.

In the next chapter, you'll train another image recognition system and use it to make a game. You'll also learn about some of the ways that ML projects can go wrong.

4

PLAYING ROCK, PAPER, SCISSORS AGAINST YOUR COMPUTER

n Chapter 3, you used ML to create an image recognition system that can sort photos of animals. You learned that we create image recognition systems by collecting examples of pictures that we want the computer to learn how to recognize.

In this chapter, you'll train an ML model to recognize the different hand shapes that you make in the game Rock, Paper, Scissors (see Figure 4-1) and then program the computer to play against you.

Figure 4-1: Playing Rock, Paper, Scissors

Let's get started!

BUILD YOUR PROJECT

For this project, you'll be taking photos of your hand, so you'll need a webcam.

TRAIN YOUR MODEL

1. Create a new ML project, name it **Rock Paper Scissors**, and set it to learn how to recognize images.

NOTE   *If you're not sure how to create an ML project, read the section "Creating a New ML Project" on page 9 in Chapter 2.*

2. Click **Train**, as shown in Figure 4-2.

Figure 4-2: Train is the first phase of an ML project.

3. Click **Add new label** to create a training bucket and enter
    the name **Rock**. Then create two more training buckets named
    Paper and **Scissors**, as shown in Figure 4-3.

*Figure 4-3: Click **Add new label** to create your training buckets.*

4. Click **webcam** in the **Rock** bucket and make a fist in front of
    your webcam, as shown in Figure 4-4.

*The first time you do this, your web browser will probably ask you
to give permission for the Machine Learning for Kids tool to use
your webcam. Click **Allow**.*

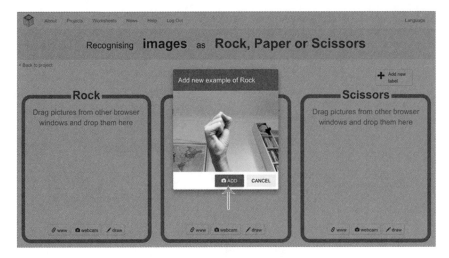

Figure 4-4: Take your first training photo using the webcam.

5. When you're ready, click **Add** (see Figure 4-4). A photo of your fist should be added to the Rock bucket, as shown in Figure 4-5.

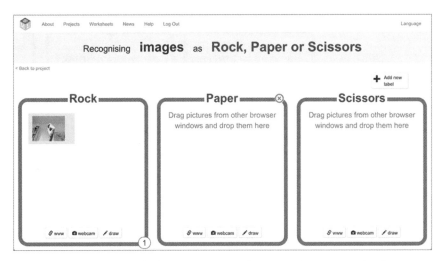

Figure 4-5: A thumbnail of your photo is shown in the training bucket.

6. Repeat steps 4 and 5 using the webcam button for the Paper and Scissors training buckets. Keep going until you have 10 photos

of a fist in the Rock bucket, 10 photos of a flat hand in the Paper bucket, and 10 photos of two fingers in the Scissors bucket, as shown in Figure 4-6.

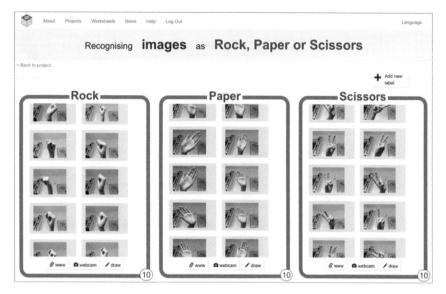

Figure 4-6: Training images for Rock, Paper, Scissors

7. Click **Back to project** in the top-left corner of the screen.
8. Click **Learn & Test**, as shown in Figure 4-7.

Figure 4-7: Learn & Test is the second phase of an ML project.

9. Click **Train new machine learning model**, as shown in Figure 4-8.

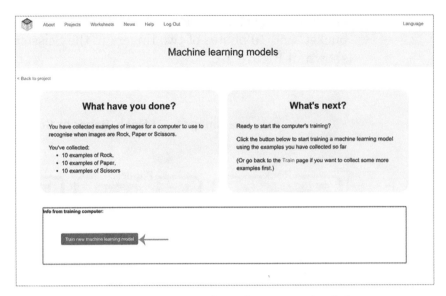

*Figure 4-8: Click **Train new machine learning model** to start training a model.*

The example photos you've taken will be used to train an ML model. The computer will learn what the photos in each bucket have in common to be able to recognize different hand shapes. This process can take a few minutes, but you can move on to the next section to start getting your game ready while you wait.

PREPARE YOUR GAME

You'll make a script in Scratch that uses your ML model to play Rock, Paper, Scissors against you. The script will use your webcam to take a picture of your hand, and your model will recognize the shape that your hand is making.

1. Click **Back to project** in the top-left corner.
2. Click **Make**.
3. Click **Scratch 3**, and then click **Open in Scratch 3** to open a new window with Scratch.

    You should see new blocks representing your ML model in the Toolbox, as shown in Figure 4-9.

4. At the top of the Scratch window, click **Project templates** as shown in Figure 4-9.

This lets you access a variety of sample and starter projects, which should save you time.

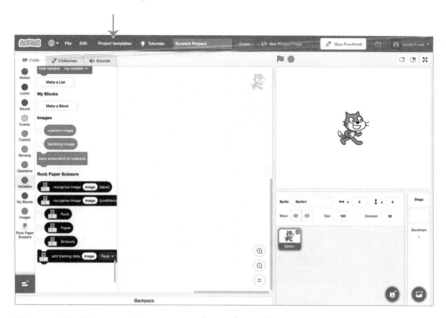

Figure 4-9: Opening Project templates from the top menu

5. Click **Rock Paper Scissors** in the list of project templates. (You can enter the name in the search field or click **Images projects** to find it more quickly.)

This template gives you most of a working Rock, Paper, Scissors game in Scratch. The following steps will show you how to add ML to the Scratch project, but before you start, try reading the code to understand how it works.

6. Click the **you** sprite and then find the **when Green Flag clicked** and **when I receive new-move** scripts, as shown in Figure 4-10.

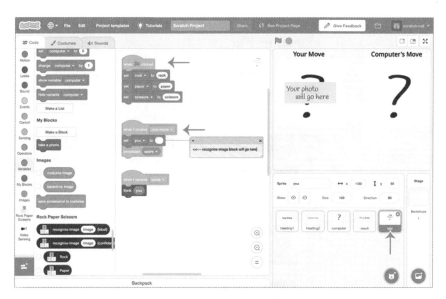

Figure 4-10: Find the scripts to modify in the **you** sprite.

7. Drag the blocks representing your **Rock, Paper, Scissors** ML training buckets into the **when Green Flag clicked** script, as shown in Figure 4-11.

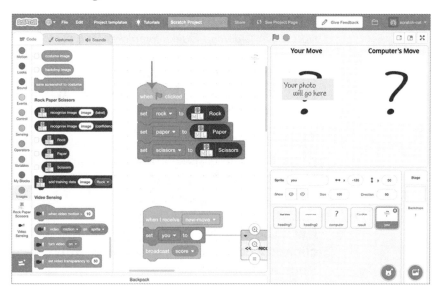

Figure 4-11: Update the **when Green Flag clicked** script with the blocks for your project.

8. Drag a **recognize image (label)** block into the **when I receive new-move** script, and then drag the **costume image** block into that block, as shown in Figure 4-12.

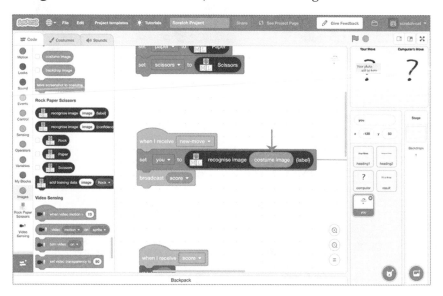

*Figure 4-12: Update the **when I receive new-move** script with the blocks for your project.*

TEST YOUR GAME

It's time to try out your project!

Click the Green Flag icon to start playing Rock, Paper, Scissors against the computer.

Hold your hand up to your webcam in the shape of a rock, paper, or scissors and press P on the keyboard to take a photo.

The computer will make a random choice from rock, paper, and scissors, and will display a cartoon to represent its move. It will use your ML model to recognize your move based on your hand shape, and then show a message saying who won (see Figure 4-13).

Figure 4-13: Playing Rock, Paper, Scissors

REVIEW AND IMPROVE YOUR PROJECT

You've trained an ML model to recognize pictures of three different hand shapes! Try experimenting with it to see what makes it work well and what makes it make mistakes.

Remember that the ML model isn't starting from an understanding of the Rock, Paper, Scissors game or the meaning of your different hand shapes. It can only learn from the patterns in the example photos that you've taken.

Imagine you took all of the rock training example photos with your hand very, very close to the webcam so that your hand looks huge, and that you took all of the scissors training example photos with your hand very, very far away from the webcam so that your hand looks tiny. A computer could assume that this size pattern was significant and learn that large hands mean "rock" and small hands mean "scissors." That means that it could recognize a photo of any large hand making any hand shape as "rock."

Now imagine you took all the rock training example photos with your hand coming in from the left, and all of the paper training example photos with your hand coming in from the right, as shown in Figure 4-14. A computer could assume this direction pattern was significant, and learn that a hand facing to the right means "rock," and a hand facing to the left means "paper." That means it could recognize a photo of any hand shape facing to the right as "rock."

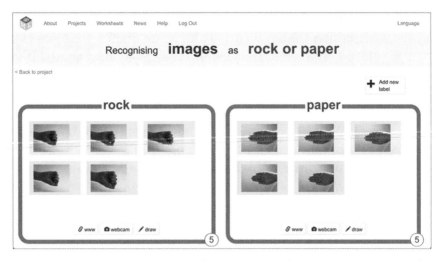

Figure 4-14: Computers can learn from unexpected patterns in the training data.

We only use the labels on the training buckets to make it easier for us to organize our projects. The computer doesn't take the labels into account when it looks for patterns in the training examples. If you hid the labels and asked a friend to guess what the photos in each set in Figure 4-14 have in common, they might say, "Those hands are all pointing to the right, and those hands are all pointing to the left." ML models work in a similar way, so they might learn to recognize misleading patterns.

The background of the photo can have a similar impact. I helped a student once who accidentally discovered this when creating this project. His face was included in all of the rock and paper training photos, but both his face and a classmate were included in all of the scissors training photos.

When he tested his project in Scratch, it seemed to do a good job of recognizing his hand shapes, until I came to stand next to him and watch. When I stood next to him, no matter the hand shape he made, his project almost always thought that he was showing scissors.

Although he hadn't realized it at first, he had trained his ML model to recognize the difference between photos with one or two people in them. It had learned to recognize photos with two people as "scissors."

If you don't want any of these misleading patterns to affect your ML model, it helps to include *variety* in your training examples. Your project will work best when your training photos include a lot of very different photos of the same subject. When taking rock training photos, make a rock shape from every different angle and direction that you can. Take some photos that are close up and large, and some that are farther away and small. If you can take photos with different backgrounds, even better. If the only thing that your rock training examples have in common is a fist hand shape, that will be the pattern the computer learns to recognize.

We'll learn more about how to confuse ML models in Chapter 14, but for now remember: *if the pictures in each training bucket have only one thing in common with each other, then that's the only pattern that the ML model will learn to recognize.*

WHAT YOU LEARNED

In this chapter, you've trained another ML model to recognize pictures. In Chapter 3, you used this to do a job: sorting photos. This time you used it to play a game of Rock, Paper, Scissors against your computer by having it recognize your hand shape. Both of these projects demonstrate *image recognition* and are good examples of how it is used every day.

You've learned that the basic approach for training computers in image recognition is to collect example photos, and you've learned the important lesson of avoiding misleading patterns in your training data to improve your results.

Computers can learn to recognize more than just what's in a picture, however, so in the next chapter you'll see some other patterns that ML models can learn.

5

RECOGNIZING MOVIE POSTERS

n the last two chapters, you collected training images to create an ML system that could identify pictures of a certain object by learning to recognize the colors, shapes, and patterns that the training images had in common.

In this chapter, you'll use the same technique to train a model to recognize the style of a picture rather than its subject. For example, if you collect examples of watercolor paintings in one training bucket, and examples of pen drawings in another training bucket, you can train an ML model to recognize whether a picture is a watercolor or a pen drawing.

The most common example of how this technique is used in real life is in search engines. Image search engines can recognize the visual style of images, allowing you to filter image search results by type (clip art, line drawings, photos, and so on). These search engines use an ML model that has been trained with a lot of examples of pictures of different styles to be able to recognize the type of each search result.

Some people use ML systems to create entirely new pictures. This involves training a computer to recognize the patterns found in works of art of a certain style, and then letting the computer use what it has learned to generate new works of art in that style. In 2018, an AI system created a painting that was auctioned as a work of art for over $400,000.

This sort of project is called *computational creativity* and has been used to create all sorts of things. AI systems have composed new pieces of music and even invented recipes and meals.

In this chapter, you'll train an ML model that can recognize the genre of a work of art based only on a picture of it.

Think about what posters for certain movie genres have in common. For example, thriller movie posters often have dark colors and large letters. Romance movie posters often have light colors and flowery letters. Science-fiction movie posters often have spaceships, stars, planets, and a black background.

We all learn these patterns, often without realizing it, so that we can recognize a movie's genre just from seeing its poster (see Figure 5-1).

In this project, you'll train the computer to recognize what works of art in a particular genre have in common. For example, do posters for action movies have anything in common? The box art for racing video games? The cover art for rap albums? You'll see whether a computer can learn to recognize these patterns so that it can identify the genre of a work of art, such as a book, based just on a picture of its cover or poster.

Figure 5-1: ML models can learn to recognize movie genres.

Let's get started!

BUILD YOUR PROJECT

Choose a type of art that can be grouped by genre and is represented by a graphical cover or poster.

For example, you could choose:

▶ Books, which are represented by book covers

▶ Movies, which are represented by movie posters

▶ Video games, which are represented by box art

▶ Music albums, which are represented by album covers

You'll need to collect pictures of your chosen works of art to be the training examples for this project. Look for websites that group books, movies, games, or albums by genre. If you've chosen books, the website for a bookstore or library is a useful source of training examples. If you've chosen music albums or video games, retailer websites are good places to try.

Next, choose a few genres that you want to train the computer to be able to recognize. Training the computer will be easier if you choose genres that are very obviously different. For example, it's easier to recognize the difference between the posters for action movies and romance movies than it is to recognize the difference between posters for action movies and adventure movies.

For the screenshots in this project, I trained an ML model to recognize three genres of movies—action, family, and drama—based on their movie posters.

Once you've chosen your type of art and genres, you can start training your model.

TRAIN YOUR MODEL

1. Create a new ML project, name it **Judge a book by its cover**, and set it to learn to recognize images.

NOTE *If you're not sure how to create an ML project, read the section "Creating a New ML Project" on page 9 in Chapter 2.*

2. Click **Train**, as shown in Figure 5-2.

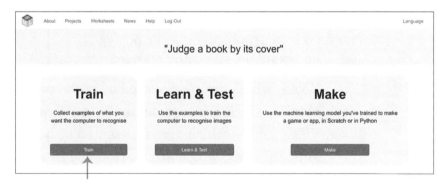

Figure 5-2: Train is the first phase of an ML project.

3. Click **Add new label**, as shown in Figure 5-3, and enter the name of your first genre.

Figure 5-3: Click **Add new label** to create training buckets for your genres.

4. Open a second window in your web browser (usually by selecting **File ▶ New Window**) and arrange your two windows side by side, as shown in Figure 5-4. In your second window, search for pictures that match your first genre.

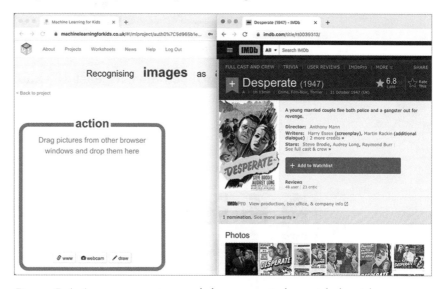

Figure 5-4: Arrange your two web browser windows side by side.

5. Drag a picture (of the book cover, movie poster, game box, or album cover) for your first genre and drop it in the training bucket in your project.

    You should see a thumbnail version of the picture in your training bucket, as shown in Figure 5-5. If you don't, try dragging and dropping the picture again.

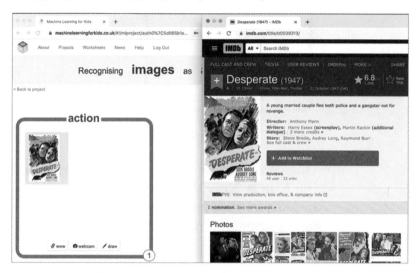

Figure 5-5: My first training example for recognizing action movies

6. Repeat step 5 until you have at least 10 examples of works of that genre, as shown in Figure 5-6.

Figure 5-6: Training examples of action movie posters

7. Repeat steps 3 through 6 for all of the genres that you want your model to be able to recognize, as shown in Figure 5-7.

   Try to collect a similar number of examples for each genre. In other words, avoid having lots of examples in one bucket but hardly any in another bucket.

Figure 5-7: Training examples for recognizing different types of movie posters

8. Click **Back to project** in the top-left corner of the screen.
9. Click **Learn & Test**, as shown in Figure 5-8.

Figure 5-8: Learn & Test is the second phase of an ML project.

10. Click **Train new machine learning model**, as shown in Figure 5-9.

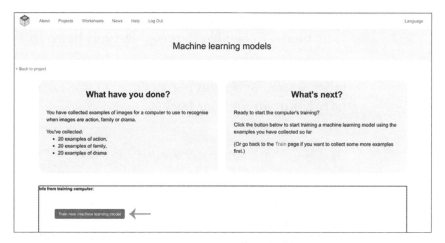

Figure 5-9: Click **Train new machine learning model** *to start the training process.*

The computer will use the examples that you've collected to look for patterns in the covers or posters from different genres. Training the model may take a few minutes, depending on how many examples you've collected, but you can move on to the next step of the project in your second web browser window while you wait.

PREPARE YOUR MODEL

You need to test whether your ML model is able to recognize a genre from a picture it hasn't seen before. To test the model, you'll save some new pictures that you haven't used for training and then create a script in Scratch to test your model with them.

1. Search for more pictures of each genre you've chosen and save them to your computer. To save the photos, right-click the image and select **Save Picture** or **Save Image As**, as shown in Figure 5-10.

NOTE   *Don't choose the same pictures you used for training the model. You want to test how good the computer is at recognizing genres, not how good it is at remembering them.*

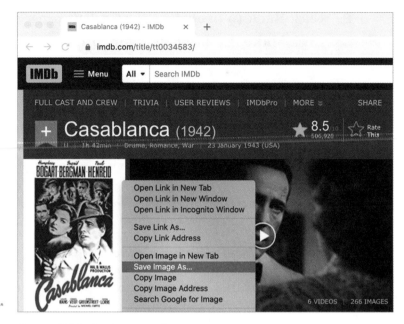

Figure 5-10: Saving test photos to your computer

Save these test photos in a folder on your computer, as shown in Figure 5-11. The more pictures you save, the more you can use to test your ML model.

Figure 5-11: Preparing test photos

2. Click **Back to project** in the top-left corner of the screen.

3. Click **Make**, as shown in Figure 5-12.

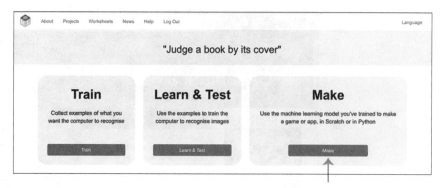

Figure 5-12: Make is the third phase of an ML project.

4. Click **Scratch 3**, and then click **Open in Scratch 3** to open a new window with Scratch.

5. Click the cat sprite (**Sprite1**) in the sprites pane at the bottom right of the screen. Then, click the **Costumes** tab at the top left.

6. Move your mouse pointer over the Choose a Costume icon in the bottom-left corner. Click **Upload Costume** and find the folder on your computer where you saved your downloaded test pictures.

7. Select all of the test photos you saved in step 1 to upload them all at once as costumes for the cat sprite.

NOTE *Make sure that you don't make each test image a separate sprite. You should only have one sprite at the bottom right, but lots of costumes on the left-hand side.*

8. Change the name of the cat sprite from **Sprite1** by entering **test images** in the Sprite text box, shown in Figure 5-13.

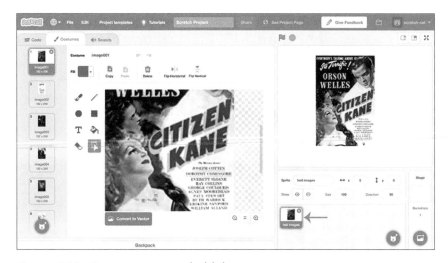

Figure 5-13: Create a sprite to hold the test images.

9. You'll need some button sprites for your Scratch project. Move your mouse pointer over the Choose a Sprite icon in the bottom-right corner.

To draw your own buttons, click **Paint** to access the drawing and coloring tools. Don't worry if you make a mistake while painting—just click the blue undo arrow next to the costume name.

If you don't like drawing, click **Choose a Sprite** and choose one from the Scratch Sprites Library, as shown in Figure 5-14.

Make one button for each of your genres.

Figure 5-14: Access the Sprites Library by clicking **Choose a Sprite**.

10. Rename your button sprites to match the genres, as shown in Figure 5-15. I named my three buttons action, family, and drama.

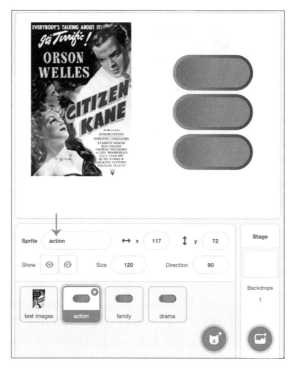

Figure 5-15: Create buttons for each genre.

11. Click the **Costumes** tab and select the Text tool (which looks like a T) to add labels to the buttons. Use the Fill tool to choose the label color. Make your labels match the names of the genres, as shown in Figure 5-16.

12. Next, you'll create three variables. Click the **Code** tab, click **Variables** in the Toolbox, and then click **Make a Variable**, as shown in Figure 5-17.

NOTE   *For all three variables, select the* **For all sprites** *option.*

Figure 5-16: I've used the Text and Fill tools to add white labels to each of the buttons.

Two of the variables count how many times you agree or disagree with the computer's decision. Name the first variable **agree** and the second variable **disagree**.

The third variable stores the computer's choice for the genre of the most recent picture. Name this variable **computer**.

*Figure 5-17: Click **Make a Variable** to create the project's three variables.*

13. Make sure the checkboxes next to the **agree** and **disagree** variables are checked. This displays them on the Stage so you can see the score while you test your project. Uncheck the box next to the **computer** variable.

14. Click the **test images** sprite (the sprite with your test pictures as costumes).

15. Copy the scripts shown in Figure 5-18.

NOTE *If you're not sure how to code in Scratch, read the section "Coding in Scratch" on page xxii in the introduction to this book.*

In the **switch costume** block, use the drop-down arrow to set the costume to the first of your test photos (in Figure 5-18, my first test photo was called *image001*).

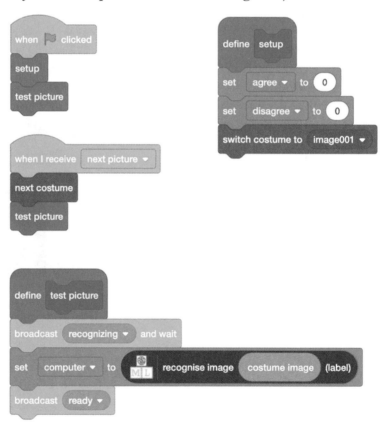

Figure 5-18: Code for recognizing the movie posters

16. Click the first of your genre button sprites, as shown in Figure 5-19.

Figure 5-19: Genre buttons

17. Copy the scripts shown in Figure 5-20, changing the **action** block to match the label of your first genre button.

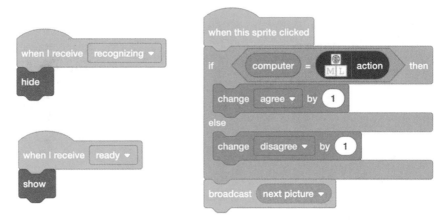

Figure 5-20: Code for the first genre button

The computer will use this code when the user clicks the button to guess the genre. If the user's choice matches what the model recognized, the agree count will increase by 1. If it doesn't match, the disagree count will increase instead.

18. Click the next genre button sprite and copy the same scripts from step 17, as shown in Figure 5-21. As before, match the genre to the label on the button. For my project, the second button was for family movies.

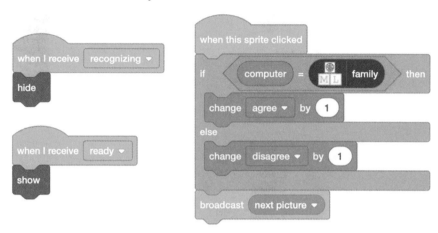

Figure 5-21: Code for the second genre button

19. Repeat step 17 until all of your genre buttons have a copy of the script, as shown in Figure 5-22.

Figure 5-22: Every genre button needs a copy of the script.

Now it's time to test your ML project!

TEST YOUR MODEL

Try to find someone else to test your ML project, since it's better for the person testing the project to not have seen the test pictures that you downloaded.

Once they click the Green Flag, Scratch will show them each test picture and ask them to decide what genre they think the work of art is. Your Scratch code will keep a count of how many times they agree with your ML model and how many times they disagree, as shown in Figure 5-23.

Figure 5-23: Testing your ML model

Ask whoever tests your project to use *only* the picture to decide what to click, even if they recognize the work of art and know something about it already.

REVIEW AND IMPROVE YOUR PROJECT

In this project, you trained an ML model to recognize the visual styles that are commonly found in images from different genres.

If your ML model performed badly, with a lot more disagrees than agrees, try adding more examples to your training buckets in the Train phase and then training a new ML model with them in the Learn & Test phase. In general, the more training examples an ML model has to learn from, the better the results.

WHAT YOU LEARNED

In this chapter, you trained another ML model to recognize pictures. In the previous two chapters, you trained image recognition systems to recognize objects in a picture. This time, you used one to recognize the style, not the subject, of a picture.

You also saw that one way we commonly measure the effectiveness of an ML system is to compare the answers that it gives to test questions with the answers people give.

In the next chapter, you'll learn about another useful image recognition application: handwriting recognition.

6
MAIL SORTING

In the last few chapters, you've been training a computer to recognize images. There are lots of useful jobs that computers can help us do if they know how to see. One such job, *optical character recognition (OCR)*, is when a computer is able to recognize a picture of a letter or number after it has seen lots of examples of that character.

A computer trained to do OCR can read the printed words in newspapers and books.

When combined with a text-to-speech system that can read the recognized words out loud, OCR is used to help visually impaired people read text that they might not be able to see for themselves.

Historians, librarians, and archivists use OCR to study historical books and printed documents. ML makes it possible to search through publications going back hundreds of years, because OCR can recognize the words.

On our roads, OCR systems recognize letters and numbers on license plates. *Automatic number plate recognition (ANPR)* is used to keep traffic flowing by enabling fast and efficient tolls and to improve road safety by recognizing when a car is driving too fast as it passes a checkpoint.

Businesses use OCR to help process forms and documents. If you fill in a form or write a check, an ML system will often use OCR to automatically recognize what you've written.

If you've traveled abroad, you may have used translation apps. You can point a smartphone at a sign or menu in a foreign language and have the phone translate that into your own language. OCR is used to recognize the words and letters in the picture.

One common use of OCR is to help sort mail, which is what we'll do in this chapter. You'll train a computer to recognize handwriting and see how OCR can be used to quickly sort letters. You'll create a mail sorting office in Scratch that can automatically sort letters by recognizing the postcode written on the envelope (see Figure 6-1).

Let's get started!

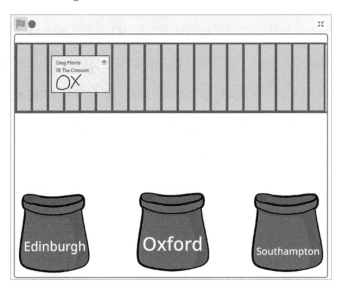

Figure 6-1: Sorting letters by recognizing the postcode

BUILD YOUR PROJECT

First, choose three big cities that you want your sorting office to be able to recognize letters for.

For my screenshots, I chose three cities in the UK: Edinburgh, Oxford, and Southampton.

Next, you need to choose some codes that can be used to identify those cities. In the UK, where I live, these are called *postcodes*. (In the United States, they're known as ZIP codes.) To make this project quicker, I used the first couple of letters of each postcode.

For my project, I used:

▶ EH as the postcode for Edinburgh addresses

▶ OX as the postcode for Oxford addresses

▶ SO as the postcode for Southampton addresses

If you're in the United States, instead of the ZIP code, you can use the postal abbreviation for the state where your cities are located. For example, you could use TX to represent Dallas addresses, or MA to represent Boston addresses.

Choose *three* cities with *three different short codes* to represent them.

TRAIN YOUR MODEL

To train the computer to recognize the postcodes you've chosen, you'll draw examples of those codes and use them to train an ML model.

1. Create a new ML project, name it **Sorting office**, and set it to learn to recognize images.

NOTE *If you're not sure how to create an ML project, read the section "Creating a New ML Project" on page 9 in Chapter 2.*

2. Click **Train**, as shown in Figure 6-2.

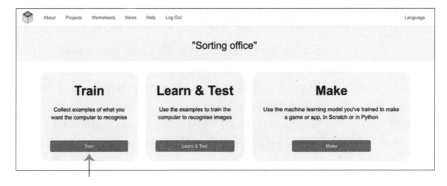

Figure 6-2: Train is the first phase of an ML project.

3. Click **Add new label**, as shown in Figure 6-3. Then enter the name of your first city.

*Figure 6-3: Click **Add new label** to create training buckets for your cities.*

4. Click **draw** at the bottom of your city training bucket, as shown in Figure 6-4.

    In the window that opens, draw in the box to write the code you want to train the computer to recognize for this city.

    When you've finished writing, click **Add**.

Figure 6-4: Click **draw** to add new examples.

Drawing the postcode is much easier if you have a touch screen, but don't worry if you have to use a mouse. Your writing doesn't need to be very neat for this project to work. Just do the best you can.

5. Repeat step 4 until you have at least 10 examples of the hand-written code for your first city, as shown in Figure 6-5.

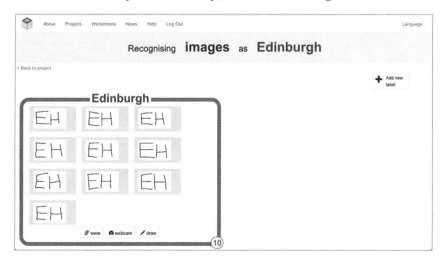

Figure 6-5: Training examples for recognizing the postcode for Edinburgh

6. Repeat steps 3 through 5 for the next two cities, until you have at least 10 examples of each city's postcode, as shown in Figure 6-6.

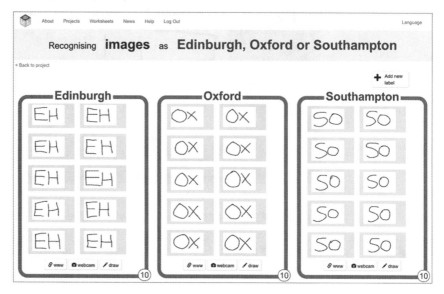

Figure 6-6: Training examples for postcodes for all three cities

7. Click **Back to project** in the top-left corner of the screen.
8. Click **Learn & Test**, as shown in Figure 6-7.

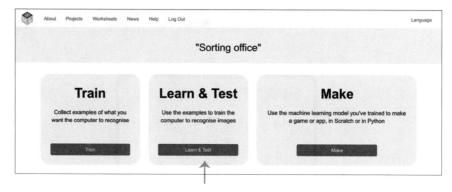

Figure 6-7: Learn & Test is the second phase of an ML project.

9. Click **Train new machine learning model**, as shown in Figure 6-8.

    The computer will use the examples that you've written to learn how to recognize the codes for different cities. As all your examples have been drawn with the same "pen" and in the same color, the computer will probably work best at recognizing codes written like that.

    The training process may take a few minutes.

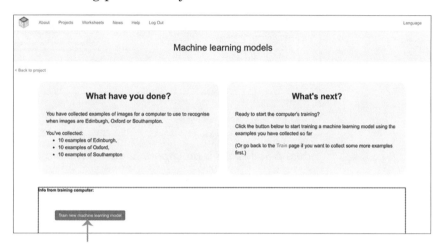

Figure 6-8: Train a new ML model to recognize postcodes.

10. It's time to test your ML model! In previous projects, you've done this by going directly to Scratch and seeing how well the computer recognizes and sorts photos you've downloaded from the internet or taken with a webcam. This time, we'll test our model here first and make sure we're happy with it before going on to Scratch.

NOTE   *When your teacher teaches you something new, they'll often test you so they can tell whether you understand what you've been taught. Testing is important in ML projects as well. After we train an ML model, we can't tell how well the training worked if we don't test the computer.*

Test your ML model by clicking **Test by drawing**, as shown in Figure 6-9. Try writing codes for your cities and see how good the computer is at recognizing what you write.

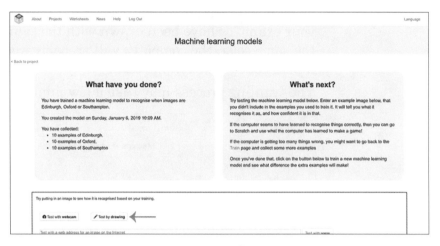

Figure 6-9: Testing is an important part of ML projects.

If you don't see the Test by drawing button, your ML model hasn't finished training yet. You may need to wait for another minute or two.

If you're not happy with how well your ML model recognizes the postcodes, you can go back to the Train phase and add more examples. In general, the more training examples you use, the better your ML model will perform. Remember to click **Train new machine learning model** again to update your ML model with the new examples.

PREPARE YOUR PROJECT

Now you'll test your ML model further by creating a virtual mail sorting office in Scratch that uses your OCR system to sort envelopes.

1. Click **Back to project** in the top-left corner of the screen.
2. Click **Make**, as shown in Figure 6-10.

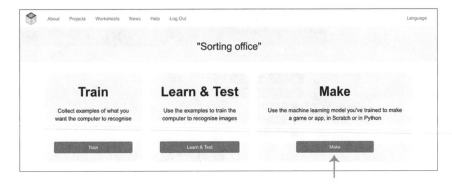

Figure 6-10: Make is the third phase of an ML project.

3. Click **Scratch 3**, and then click **Open in Scratch 3** to open a new window with Scratch. You should see a new section in the Toolbox, as shown in Figure 6-11, containing blocks from your Sorting Office project.

Figure 6-11: Scratch 3 with your ML model blocks

4. In the top of the Scratch window, click **Project templates**, as shown in Figure 6-12.

This lets you access sample projects and starter code to help save you time.

Figure 6-12: Click **Project templates** in the top menu.

5. Click the **Sorting Office** template, as shown in Figure 6-13.

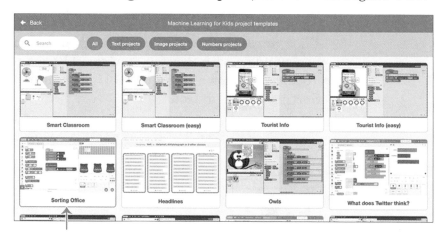

Figure 6-13: The Sorting Office project template

6. Click the **Stage** backdrop, as shown in Figure 6-14.

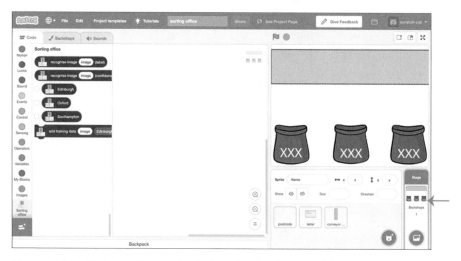

Figure 6-14: Click the **Stage** backdrop for the Sorting Office project.

7. Click the **Backdrops** tab, as shown in Figure 6-15.

8. Use the Text tool to edit the labels on the mail sacks. Edit all three sacks so that their labels match the names of the cities you chose. If you can't fit the city's whole name, you can just use the postcode.

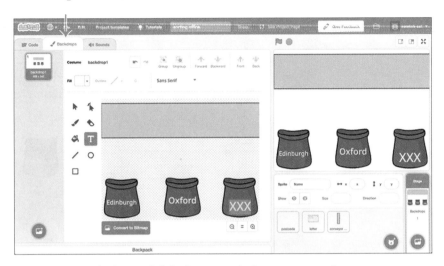

Figure 6-15: Edit the sack labels to match the cities you chose.

9. Click the **postcode** sprite and then click the **Costumes** tab, as shown in Figure 6-16.

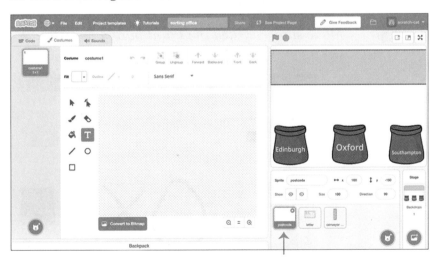

Figure 6-16: You'll find the postcode sprite in the sprites list.

10. Use the Paintbrush tool to write the letters for one of your cities onto the canvas.

You'll get the best results if you match the line style to the training examples that you wrote before, so set **Fill** to black and the line width to about **20**, as shown in Figure 6-17.

Figure 6-17: Set the paint tools to match your training examples.

11. When you've finished, click the **Paint** button in the *bottom-left* corner to add a new costume, as shown in Figure 6-18.

NOTE *Make sure you click the Paint button for creating a new costume, not a new sprite.*

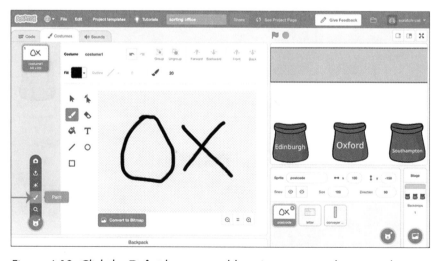

*Figure 6-18: Click the **Paint** button to add new costumes to the postcode sprite.*

12. Repeat steps 10 and 11 until you have several costumes in the postcode sprite. Draw each city's code multiple times, as shown in Figure 6-19.

Don't worry if you make a mistake while drawing—just click the blue undo arrow next to the costume name.

Figure 6-19: Draw several test costumes in the postcode sprite.

13. Click the **Code** tab and find the **when Green Flag clicked** script, as shown in Figure 6-20.

You might need to scroll around to find this script. It should be in the top left of the Code Area.

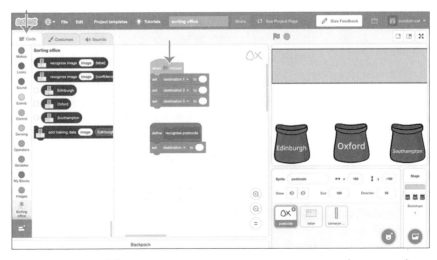

Figure 6-20: Find the **when Green Flag clicked** script in the postcode sprite.

NOTE *You should still be on the **postcode** sprite. If you clicked a different sprite, click back on the **postcode** sprite now.*

14. Drag the blocks with the names of your cities into the **when Green Flag clicked** script, as shown in Figure 6-21.

    There's more than one when Green Flag clicked script in the Code Area, so scroll around until you find the one that looks like the script in Figure 6-21.

    It's important that you match the order with the names that you wrote on the mail sacks on the backdrop. The left sack is destination1. The middle sack is destination2. The right sack is destination3.

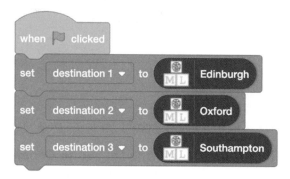

Figure 6-21: Identify the names of your cities for the project.

15. Find the **recognise postcode** script in the Code Area. It should be immediately beneath the when Green Flag clicked script from the previous step, still on the **postcode** sprite.

16. Drag the **recognise image (label)** block into the **recognise postcode** script, and then drag the **costume image** block into the **recognise image (label)** block, as shown in Figure 6-22.

Figure 6-22: Script for recognizing the postcode on an envelope

TEST YOUR PROJECT

It's time to try sorting some letters!

Click the Green Flag icon to watch your ML model at work.

The conveyor belt at the top of the screen will begin running, and the letters with the postcodes you've written will start to scroll by, as shown in Figure 6-23.

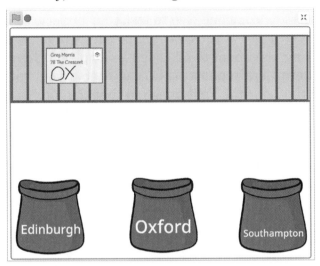

Figure 6-23: A test envelope on the conveyor belt

The envelope will zoom in while your ML model tries to recognize what you've written.

Once it has classified your picture, the script will send the envelope to the corresponding mail sack, as shown in Figure 6-24.

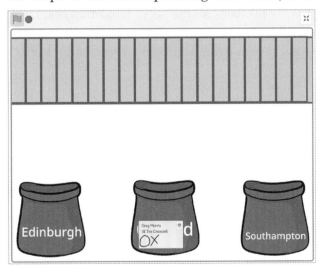

Figure 6-24: Test results for recognizing a postcode

REVIEW AND IMPROVE YOUR PROJECT

You've trained an ML model to recognize handwriting on an envelope, and you've created a project in Scratch that uses OCR to automatically sort letters!

How could you improve your project?

Try getting someone else to test your project. Can it recognize their handwriting? If the model makes a lot of mistakes with their handwriting, ask them to add some examples to your training buckets in the Train phase. (Make sure that you train a new ML model in the Learn & Test phase so that the computer can learn from both of your examples.)

The wider the variety of examples you use to train the computer, the better the ML model should be at recognizing different handwriting styles.

What else could you do to improve your project?

WHAT YOU LEARNED

Sorting mail is a common use of *optical character recognition*. Large sorting offices around the world use OCR systems to recognize and sort letters in a fraction of a second. Your project just recognized a postcode, but real-world multiline optical character readers can recognize several lines of an address. The basic idea is very similar, and it helps make large-scale mail sorting efficient and practical.

All of your projects so far have used images, but computers can be trained to recognize many different types of data. In the next chapter, you'll train an ML model to recognize text!

7

INSULTING A COMPUTER

n this chapter, we'll look at how computers can be trained to recognize different tones and emotion in written text, a technique known as *sentiment analysis*.

Imagine you need to write a few sentences to say that you are going to the zoo tomorrow.

Think about what you might write if you're super happy and excited about going. You love the zoo, and you can't wait to go. What sorts of words would you use? Would your excitement affect the way you write the sentences?

Now think of what you might write if you're angry about having to go. You hate zoos, there are other things that you'd rather be doing tomorrow, and you're annoyed that someone is making you go. How might that show up in your writing? Would your annoyance make you use different sorts of words than you would if you were happy about going? Would you phrase your sentences differently?

Both of these paragraphs would have the same basic meaning (that you are going to the zoo tomorrow), but their tone and sentiment would be different. Computers can be trained to recognize the patterns in how we write when we're annoyed compared with how we write when we're happy. With enough examples of text demonstrating different emotions and sentiment, you can train an ML model to identify the emotion or tone in a new piece of writing based on patterns in vocabulary and grammar that the computer learns to recognize.

ML systems that are trained to recognize sentiment and emotion in text can be used to understand how people feel about things. For example, businesses use sentiment analysis to find out what people think about their products or services by pointing their ML model at millions of blogs, forums, newsgroups, and social media posts—far more than they could ever read themselves. Sentiment analysis tells them how much of that feedback seems positive and how much seems negative, and what the most common complaints and criticisms are.

Sentiment analysis isn't just applied to massive amounts of text across the whole internet, though. Companies will often use it to help sort and prioritize customer support letters and emails, replying first to the letters and emails that sound the angriest or most annoyed.

Similarly, companies use sentiment analysis on their own internal discussions as a way of estimating how happy their employees are and if there are any issues or concerns that need attention.

In this chapter, you'll train an ML model to recognize the sentiment expressed by two different types of text: compliments and insults.

BUILD YOUR PROJECT

In this project, you'll create a character that reacts to a message you type (see Figure 7-1). If you give the character a compliment, it will look happy. If you insult it, it will look sad.

Figure 7-1: Recognizing compliments and insults

PREPARE YOUR GAME

First, start by designing your character. For my screenshots, I drew a simple face. You can draw anything you like, as long as you can tell if it is happy or sad. You could make an animal, a robot, an alien, or anything else you can think of.

1. Go to *https://machinelearningforkids.co.uk/scratch3/* to start a new Scratch project.
2. Click the **Costumes** tab, as shown in Figure 7-2.

Figure 7-2: Designing a character in the Costumes tab

3. Move your mouse pointer over the cat face icon at the bottom left of the screen to see the choices for adding a costume, as shown in Figure 7-3.

Figure 7-3: Adding a new costume

If you'd like to draw your own character, click **Paint**. For my screenshots, I drew a simple green alien character by drawing a few colored circles and adding some hair (see Figure 7-4).

If you'd prefer not to draw the character yourself, you have a few other options. If your computer has a webcam and you want to use a photo of your face, click **Camera**. Or, to use a picture you've saved on the computer (such as one you downloaded from the internet), click **Upload Costume**. To pick a costume from the Scratch Costume Library instead, click **Choose a Costume**.

No matter which choice you make, you should see the character on the canvas after this step.

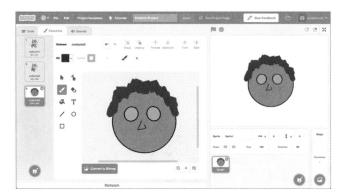

Figure 7-4: Drawing your character

4. Right-click the character costume in the costume pane and click **duplicate**, as shown in Figure 7-5. You'll need three copies of it.

Make sure you duplicate the costume, not the sprite. You want one sprite with three different costume expressions, not three different sprites.

Figure 7-5: Duplicating a costume

5. Rename each copy of the character by clicking it in the costume pane and then typing the new name in the **Costume** text box above the canvas, as shown in Figure 7-6. Name them **waiting**, **feeling happy**, and **feeling sad**.

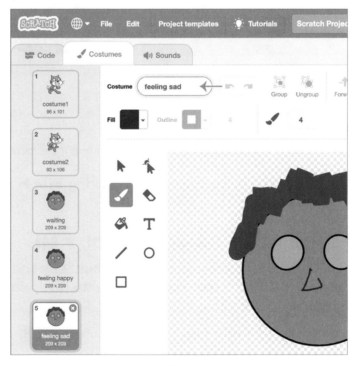

Figure 7-6: Renaming your character costumes

6. Click each character costume in the costume pane and draw an expression that matches its name, as shown in Figure 7-7.

   The feeling happy costume should look happy. If it's a face, you could make it smile. If it's an animal, you could change the position of its tail or ears. Or you could just draw the character holding up a sign that says how it feels.

   The feeling sad costume should look sad. If it's a face, you could draw a frown or tears.

   The waiting costume will be used while your character is waiting for you to say something to it, so it should be neither happy nor sad.

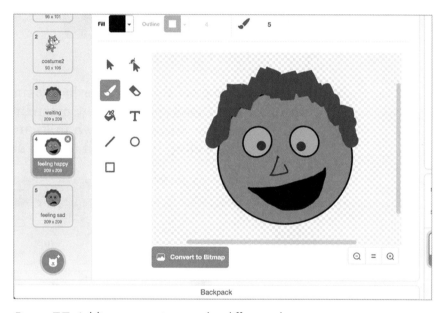

Figure 7-7: Adding expressions to the different character costumes

7. Save your Scratch project by clicking **File ▶ Save to your computer**.

CODE YOUR GAME WITHOUT ML

It's useful to see the difference ML makes by trying to code this AI project without it first. But you can skip this part if you'd rather go straight to using ML.

1. Click the **Code** tab, as shown in Figure 7-8.

Figure 7-8: The Code tab

2. Copy the script shown in Figure 7-9.

NOTE *If you're not sure how to code in Scratch, read the section "Coding in Scratch" on page xxii in the introduction.*

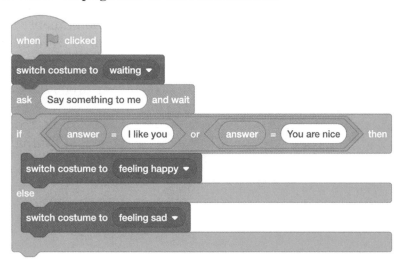

Figure 7-9: Coding the project without ML

3. Save your project, using **File ▶ Save to your computer**.

4. Test your project by clicking the Green Flag icon. Your character will ask you to say something to it. Type **I like you** or

You are nice, and your character will look happy. If you type anything else, your character will look sad.

Now type **You are lovely**. Why doesn't your character look happy?

What would you need to change about your code so it would recognize "I like you" and "You are nice" *and* "You are lovely" as compliments?

Do you think you can write a script that includes *every possible way* of phrasing every possible compliment and insult?

In Chapter 1, I said that ML is not the only way to create an AI system. Here you've created an AI program using a *rules-based* approach. You can see why, although rules-based techniques like this are still used for some very simple AI projects, ML is the preferred approach for more complicated projects. We'll train our project that way next, and later in the chapter we'll see how the ML code performs compared to the rules-based code.

TRAIN YOUR MODEL

To train the computer to recognize compliments and insults, you'll collect examples of both and use them to train an ML model.

1. Create a new ML project, name it **Make me happy**, and set it to learn to recognize text in your preferred language.

NOTE   *If you're not sure how to create an ML project, read the section "Creating a New ML Project" on page 9 in Chapter 2.*

2. Click **Train**, as shown in Figure 7-10.

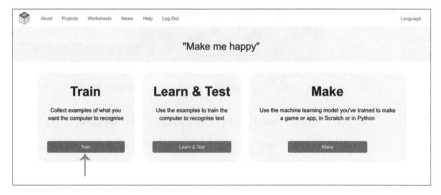

Figure 7-10: Train is the first phase of an ML project.

3. Click **Add new label**, as shown in Figure 7-11. Name this training bucket **compliments**. Then, create a second training bucket and name it **insults**.

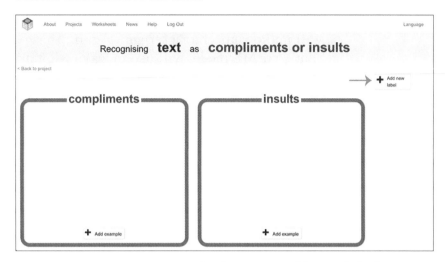

*Figure 7-11: Prepare two training buckets using **Add new label**.*

4. Click **Add example** in the **compliments** bucket, as shown in Figure 7-12, and type the best compliment that you can think of.

Repeat this step to add at least five examples of compliments that will make your character happy. These are the examples your ML model will use to learn what a compliment looks like, so try to think of a wide variety.

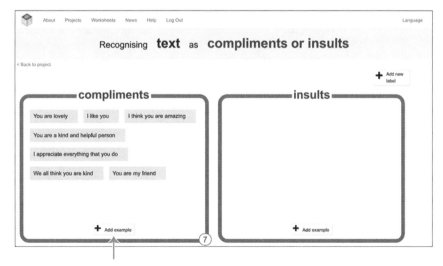

Figure 7-12: Training examples for recognizing compliments

5. Click **Add example** in the **insults** bucket, as shown in Figure 7-13, and type the meanest, cruelest insult that you can think of.

Repeat this step to add at least *five* examples of insults that will make your character sad. Again, these are the examples that your ML model will use to learn what an insult looks like, so try to come up with several variations.

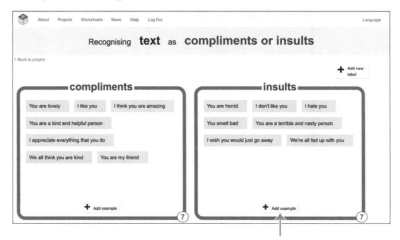

Figure 7-13: Training examples for recognizing insults

6. Click **Back to project** in the top-left corner of the screen.
7. Click **Learn & Test**.
8. Click **Train new machine learning model**, as shown in Figure 7-14.

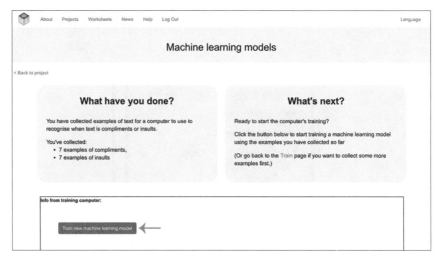

Figure 7-14: Training a new ML model

The computer will use the examples you've just created to learn how to recognize compliments and insults.

To do so, it will look for patterns in the examples you've written. It will learn from both the words you chose and the way you phrased the sentences. Then, it will use these patterns to recognize the meaning of messages we'll send to it in the next steps.

Training the model might take a minute, but you'll notice that it's much quicker than the image classifiers that you have been training in the previous chapters. Learning to recognize patterns in text is much easier for computers than learning to recognize patterns in images.

9. Test your ML model by typing a compliment or insult into the **Test** box, as shown in Figure 7-15.

   It's important that you test it with examples you have not included in the training buckets. You're testing how well the computer can recognize new examples that it's never seen before, not how well it remembers the examples you've already given it.

   If your model gets things wrong, go back to the Train phase and add more examples. Then, come back to the Learn & Test phase and train a new ML model.

   Keep going until you're happy with how the computer performs. In the next chapter, you'll learn better ways to test ML models, but for now, simply trying out the model a few times is a good start.

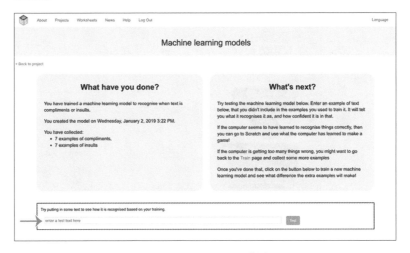

Figure 7-15: Testing is an important part of ML.

CODE YOUR GAME WITH ML

Now that you have an ML model that can recognize compliments and insults, you'll modify your earlier project to use your ML model instead of the rules you used before.

1. Click **Back to project** in the top-left corner of the screen.
2. Click **Make**, as shown in Figure 7-16.

Figure 7-16: Once you're happy with your ML model, it's time to make something with it!

3. Click **Scratch 3**, and then click **Open in Scratch 3** to open a new window with Scratch.

You should see new blocks representing your ML model in the Toolbox, as shown in Figure 7-17.

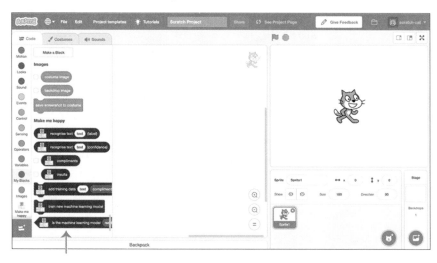

Figure 7-17: Scratch will open with a new set of blocks for your project.

4. Open your saved project by clicking **File ▶ Load from your computer**, as shown in Figure 7-18.

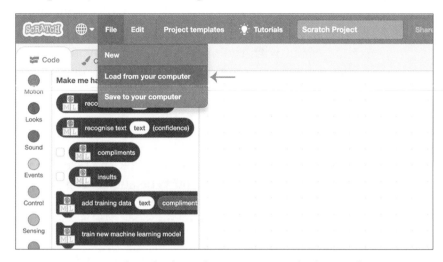

Figure 7-18: Open the rules-based project you worked on earlier.

5. If you created the rules-based script earlier, update it to match Figure 7-19. If you skipped the rules-based approach to the project, create the whole script shown in Figure 7-19.

NOTE   *If you're not sure how to code in Scratch, read the section "Coding in Scratch" on page xxii in the introduction.*

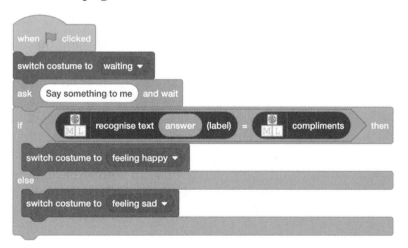

Figure 7-19: Coding the project using ML

In this script, your character will ask you to say something to it. The script uses your ML model to recognize whether the message you type is a compliment or an insult. It will display one of the costumes you've drawn based on what it's recognized, making it look like your character is reacting to whether you're complimenting or insulting it!

If you coded this project earlier without ML, compare this script with the previous one. Can you see how ML makes it easier to create a project that can react to a wider variety of possible messages?

TEST YOUR GAME

It's time to test your project. Click the Green Flag and try typing a few messages. Even if you type something you didn't use for training, hopefully the character will correctly react to your message. If it doesn't, you can always go back to the Train phase to add more examples and then train a new ML model.

You've successfully created a character that has learned to recognize and react to compliments and insults you give it!

REVIEW AND IMPROVE YOUR PROJECT

Let's look at a few ways you could improve this project.

USING SPEECH INPUT INSTEAD OF TYPING

What about changing your project so that you can say your compliments and insults aloud instead of typing them?

You'll need a microphone on your computer to be able to use speech input, and you'll need to add the Speech to Text extension from the Scratch Extensions Library. To access the Extensions Library, click the Add Extension icon (it looks like two blocks with a plus sign, +) at the bottom of the Toolbox. This library contains additional blocks you can use in your projects.

Find and click the **Speech to Text** extension to add those blocks to your Toolbox, and then update your script to look like Figure 7-20.

NOTE *At the time of writing, the Scratch Speech to Text extension can be used only in the Google Chrome web browser.*

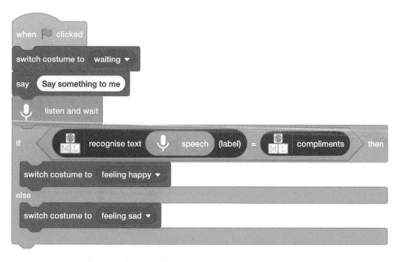

Figure 7-20: The Make me happy project using speech recognition

Speech recognition is another application of ML. For this improvement, you aren't training the speech ML model yourself, you're using a model that someone else has trained for you. But the basic principle behind how the speech blocks were created is similar to how you created the typed examples of compliments and insults.

What else could you do to improve your project?

RECOGNIZING SPEECH THAT ISN'T A COMPLIMENT OR INSULT

Type **What is the time?** to your character. It might think that this question is a compliment and look happy. Or it might identify it as an insult and look sad.

Neither of those reactions is really the right thing to do. You could update your code so that it doesn't react at all when it gets messages that aren't a compliment or an insult.

When you tested your ML model in the Learn & Test phase, you may have noticed the confidence score showing how confident the computer is that it has recognized the message.

Try typing **What is the time?** again now, as shown in Figure 7-21.

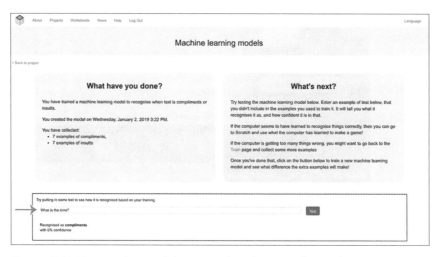

Figure 7-21: Testing the confidence in classifying "What is the time?"

You should see that this message gets a very low confidence score. This is the ML model's way of telling you that it didn't recognize the text. It's saying that in all of the training examples you've given it, it hasn't seen anything like that before, so it wasn't able to recognize whether the message was a compliment or insult.

My ML model had a confidence score of 0 in its classifying of "What is the time?" Your ML model might have scored a bit higher, depending on how you trained it. For example, if you included a lot of questions like "What is wrong with you?" in your insults bucket, your ML model might have 10 percent confidence that "What is the time?" is an insult, just because it is a question. That would still be useful information, as it's telling you that there's a 90 percent chance that the message isn't an insult. It's saying that the message had some similarities to patterns that it recognizes from the insults it learned from, but that it isn't able to *confidently* identify the message as an insult.

Experiment with different test sentences that aren't compliments or insults to see what sort of confidence scores you get. Compare these with the confidence scores you get when you test your ML model on messages that really are compliments and insults.

What sort of confidence score does your ML model give when it correctly recognizes an actual compliment or insult?

You can use the confidence score in your Scratch project, as shown in Figure 7-22.

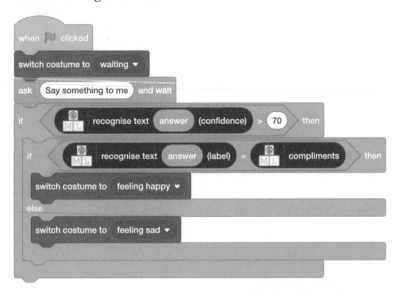

Figure 7-22: Using confidence scores in your code

This script will make the character react only if the ML model is at least 70 percent confident that it has recognized the message you give it. Otherwise, the script will ignore the message.

You'll need to change the 70 to a percentage that works for your ML model, based on your own testing.

Is there anything else you could do to improve your project?

LEARNING FROM MISTAKES

When someone is using an ML system, they'll often know if the computer has made a mistake. One way to improve your ML project is to let it learn from those mistakes.

Give the user a way to tell the project if the ML model makes a mistake. It could be a button to click, or a text box where they type "yes" or "no" in response to being asked, "Did I get that right?"

The script shown in Figure 7-23 will ask if the ML model is correct. If you type "no," the text the computer didn't recognize correctly will be added to the training examples. After every five new training examples, a new ML model is trained.

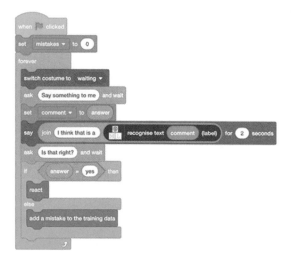

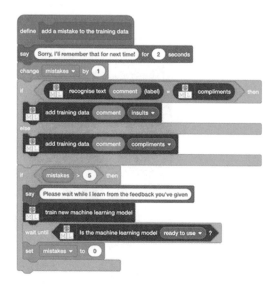

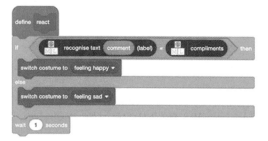

Figure 7-23: An example of learning from mistakes

Training your model to learn from mistakes will make it smarter the longer you use it. Think of how you'd like to tell your character when it has misunderstood you, and use a script like this so it can learn from your feedback.

WHAT YOU LEARNED

In this chapter, you learned about *sentiment analysis*, the use of ML to recognize the tone and emotion in text. You learned how businesses and organizations use sentiment analysis to get valuable insight and feedback from customers on the internet, prioritize customer service responses, and measure employee satisfaction.

You discovered that ML is a much better approach to building AI systems for complex projects than a simple rules-based method. You also learned how confidence scores can tell you how sure an ML model is of the predictions it's making, and saw how you could improve your ML models by helping them learn from their mistakes.

In the next chapter, you'll use an approach similar to sentiment analysis to train a model to recognize different styles of writing.

8

RECOGNIZING LANGUAGE IN NEWSPAPERS

n the last chapter, you saw that computers can be trained to recognize different characteristics of writing. For that project, you trained an ML model to recognize compliments and insults. Computers can also learn to recognize lots of other styles of writing as well.

For example, you can train an ML model to recognize the differences between formal writing and casual writing in the same way—by training it to recognize patterns in the words that people choose and the phrasing they use.

Different newspapers and news websites use words and phrases in different ways to describe the same stories. In this chapter, you'll train a computer to recognize the way that language is used in media by creating an ML model that can identify the type of newspaper a headline has come from (see Figure 8-1).

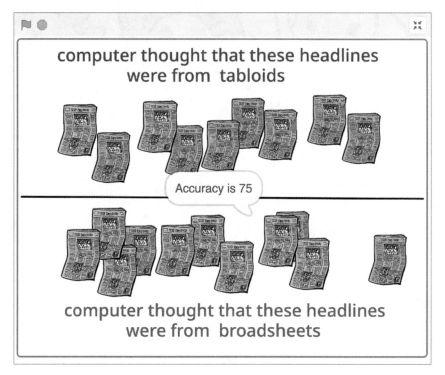

Figure 8-1: Recognizing headlines from newspapers

Let's get started!

BUILD YOUR PROJECT

The aim of this project is to see whether a computer can learn to recognize the way that newspapers use language. For the screenshots in this chapter, I trained an ML model to recognize headlines from *tabloids* (smaller newspapers with gossip stories and lots of photos) compared to *broadsheets* (traditional, full-size newspapers with more serious articles).

You can do the same topic as well, or you can design your own project. If you choose to design your own project, you should choose *one* characteristic to train the computer to recognize. There are lots of things that you could investigate. For example, you could base your project on the following:

UK newspapers (versus US newspapers)   Do American newspapers use language differently than British newspapers?

Headlines in the summer (compared with winter headlines) Are the front-page headlines written differently at different times of year?

National newspapers (versus local newspapers)   Are the headlines in national papers written differently than the headlines in your local paper?

Weekend headlines (versus weekday headlines)   Do newspapers use language differently on work and school days than on the weekend?

Articles from two different newspapers   If you pick two specific newspapers, can you train the computer to recognize an article from one of them?

Headlines from the 1950s (compared with headlines today)   Are headlines written differently today from how they used to be?

You'll need examples of the types of newspaper articles or headlines that you want to train the ML model to recognize. There are lots of websites you can use to find examples. Here are a few suggestions:

https://www.thepaperboy.com/

https://www.ukpressonline.co.uk/

https://www.time.com/vault/

Think about what comparison you would find interesting and then see if you can find enough examples to make it easy to do. You'll need two groups to train the ML model:

▶ Examples of the type of newspaper article/headline that you want the model to recognize

▶ Examples of newspaper articles/headlines that *don't* have that characteristic

Try to change only one characteristic in the second group. For example, the category *headlines from UK tabloids in the 1970s* has three variables: country (UK), newspaper type (tabloids), and time period (1970s). What would you put in the second group?

You could fill it with examples of headlines from US tabloids in the 1970s, so the computer learns to recognize the difference between 1970s UK and US tabloid headlines. Or, you could fill it with examples of headlines from UK tabloids from today, so the computer learns to recognize the difference between UK tabloid headlines from the 1970s and now.

What you should *not* do is use, for example, headlines from current US broadsheets. That would change all three variables, which would make it harder for the model to recognize a consistent pattern.

NOTE *Choose* one thing *that you want the computer to learn to recognize and try to keep everything else the same in both groups of examples.*

As another example, if you want to train the computer to recognize the way that articles are written in the *Daily Times*, in the second group you could include articles from different newspapers from the same day. Even better, you could try to pick articles about the same subject. Then your ML model won't be learning to recognize the article subject, but rather the patterns in the way the *Daily Times* describes the same subjects.

To train my ML model to recognize headlines from tabloids, I compared examples of tabloid headlines with headlines from broadsheet newspapers. Here's what I kept the same:

▶ I used newspapers from the *same time period*: March 2015 through April 2015.

▶ I used the *same section* of each newspaper: the headline in the biggest text on the front page.

▶ I used the *same type* of newspapers: national, weekday newspapers.

▶ I used newspapers from the *same country*: the UK.

TRAIN YOUR MODEL

1. Create a new ML project, name it **Newspapers**, and set it to learn to recognize text in your preferred language.

NOTE *If you're not sure how to create an ML project, read the section "Creating a New ML Project" on page 9 in Chapter 2.*

2. Click **Train**, as shown in Figure 8-2.

Figure 8-2: Train is the first phase of an ML project.

3. Click **Add new label**, as shown in Figure 8-3, to create training buckets for the two groups that you want to compare in your project.

   For my project, I used tabloid and broadsheet.

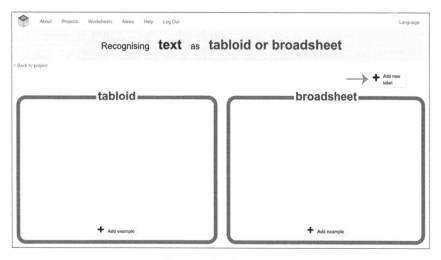

Figure 8-3: Create training buckets for the two groups to compare.

4. Find and copy an example of your first group. This will depend on what you're doing your project on. It could be a newspaper headline if you're doing a project on headlines. It could be the first paragraph of an article if you're comparing the way that different newspapers write articles about the same topic.

For my project, I copied headlines from a website that has the front page for national newspapers in the UK.

5. Click **Add example** in each of your training buckets, as shown in Figure 8-4, and paste in the examples that you found.

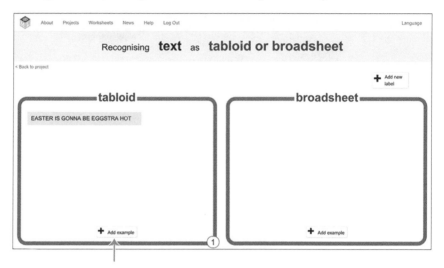

Figure 8-4: First training example for the Newspapers project

6. Repeat steps 4 and 5 until you've got at least 20 examples in each training bucket, as shown in Figure 8-5.

7. Click **Back to project** in the top-left corner of the screen.

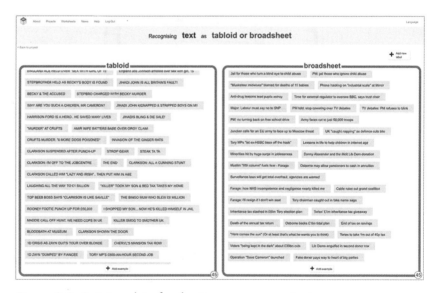

Figure 8-5: Training data for the Newspapers project

8. Click **Learn & Test**, as shown in Figure 8-6.

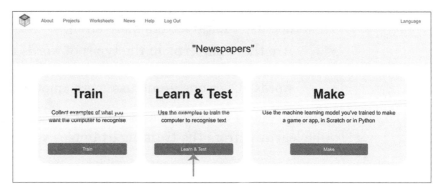

Figure 8-6: Learn & Test is the second phase of an ML project.

9. Click **Train new machine learning model**, as shown in Figure 8-7.

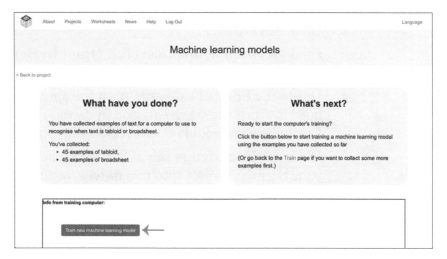

Figure 8-7: Click **Train new machine learning model** to start the training.

The computer might take a minute to learn from the examples that you've collected. While you wait, consider these questions:

▶ Did you spot any patterns between your two groups of examples while you were copying them into your training buckets?

▶ Are there particular topics or subjects that are covered more often in one group than the other?

▶ Are there particular words, terms, or phrases that are used more in one group than in the other group?

▶ Are there differences in the way sentences are structured? Does one group have longer sentences than the other? Does one use capital letters more often?

▶ Are there patterns in the types of words that are used? For example, does one group use simpler language or shorter words? Does one group use more emotional words?

Try to guess what sorts of patterns that your ML model might be learning from the training examples you've given it.

PREPARE YOUR PROJECT

In the projects that you've made so far, you've tested your ML models by trying them out. In this chapter, you'll see a few of the ways that ML projects are formally tested in the real world.

1. Click **Back to project** in the top-left corner of the screen.

2. Click **Make**.

3. Click **Scratch 3**, and then click **Open in Scratch 3** to open a new window with Scratch.

4. Delete the **Sprite1** cat sprite from the sprites list, as you won't need it. Click the trash can icon in its top-right corner. The Costumes tab should now be replaced by the Backdrops tab.

5. Click the **Backdrops** tab and draw a background that divides your Scratch project into two halves, as shown in Figure 8-8.

   The *top half* will be for newspapers that *match* what you've trained the ML model to recognize.

   The *bottom half* will be for newspapers that *don't match* what you've trained the ML model to recognize.

   Choose a color for each half. I used red for the top half, and blue for the bottom half.

   Draw a line between the two halves to divide the space.

   You should end up with something like Figure 8-8.

6. Add a sprite by moving your mouse pointer over the Choose a Sprite icon (the cat face) at the bottom right of the screen. This sprite will represent the newspaper headlines that your ML model should recognize, so give it a suitable name in both the **Costume** text field above the canvas and in the **Sprite** text field at the bottom right.

To draw your own newspaper, select **Paint**.

To upload a picture of a newspaper you've saved to the computer, click **Upload Sprite**.

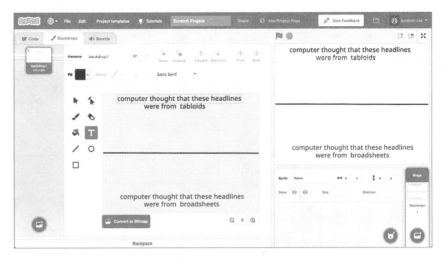

Figure 8-8: Prepare the backdrop for the Newspapers project.

7. Click the **Costumes** tab and use the paint tools to color the newspaper to match the top half of the backdrop.

For my project, I drew a red newspaper sprite to represent headlines from tabloids and gave it the name tabloid, as shown in Figure 8-9.

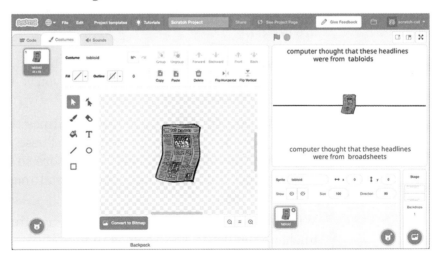

Figure 8-9: Draw the first newspaper sprite.

8. Click the **Code** tab, click **Variables** in the Toolbox, and then click **Make a List**, as shown in Figure 8-10.

Make sure **for all sprites** is selected, and name your list after what you've trained your ML model to recognize.

For my project, I created a list called tabloid headlines.

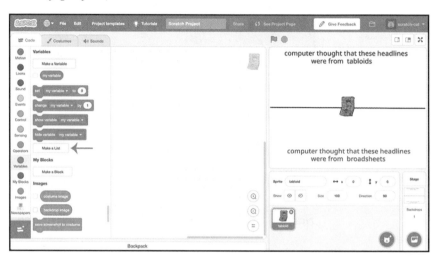

Figure 8-10: Create a list for the first set of headlines.

9. Type at least 10 examples into the list, as shown in Figure 8-11. Click the plus button in the bottom-left corner of the list to add a new line. You can drag the equal sign in the bottom-right corner to make the list wider, which can make it easier to see what you are typing.

The text you type into this list should be examples of newspaper headlines or articles that fit what you've trained the ML model to recognize.

It's important that these are new headlines that you haven't already used in the training examples. These should be headlines that the computer hasn't seen before so that you can properly test if it can recognize new headlines, not simply remember them.

When you've finished typing your test headlines into the list, uncheck the list in the Toolbox to hide it from the Stage.

Figure 8-11: Test examples for the first group

10. Click the **Code** tab and copy the scripts shown in Figure 8-12.

Replace the tabloid block with the label for whatever you've trained the computer to recognize in your project.

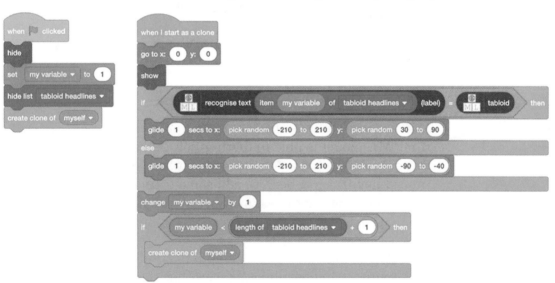

Figure 8-12: First code scripts for the Newspapers project

This script will go through each of my tabloid headlines, and if the ML model recognizes it as a tabloid headline, it will move that headline to the top half of the screen. Otherwise, it will move the headline to the bottom half of the screen.

You did something similar in Chapter 3 when you sorted animal sprites based on an ML model recognizing what the sprite looked like. This time, you're sorting sprites based on the ML model recognizing some text in your list.

11. Click the Green Flag and watch your script run.

How did your ML model do? It will probably get some answers wrong, but hopefully it will get most right. You can see how my ML model performed in Figure 8-13.

Figure 8-13: First test for the Newspapers project

But you can't tell just from this grouping of newspaper sprites if my ML model is able to distinguish tabloid headlines from broadsheet headlines. Maybe it recognizes almost anything as tabloid headlines. I need to add some examples of broadsheet headlines to my list to know if my model would recognize them as well.

12. Follow the instructions from step 6 to create a new sprite, this time representing headlines/articles that should go in the *bottom half* of the backdrop you created. Color the sprite to match the color you chose for the bottom half of the screen when you drew the backdrop, and give the sprite and costume a name that fits what you're training the model to recognize.

For my project, I drew a blue newspaper sprite to represent broadsheet headlines and named it broadsheet, as shown in Figure 8-14.

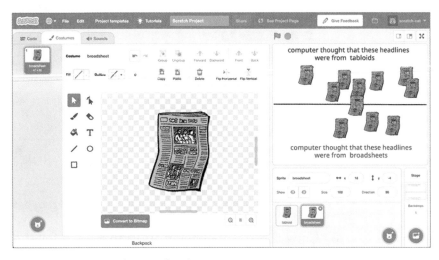

Figure 8-14: Second sprite for the Newspapers project

13. On the **Code** tab, click **Variables** in the Toolbox and then click **Make a List**. Fill this list with at least 10 examples of headlines/articles that should go in the bottom half of the backdrop.

    As before, make sure **for all sprites** is selected and name the list to match your second group.

    For my project, I created a list named broadsheet headlines and filled it with 10 examples of broadsheet headlines, as shown in Figure 8-15.

    When you've typed your test headlines into the list, uncheck the list in the Toolbox to hide the list in the Stage.

14. Create a variable to count these headlines by clicking your second newspaper sprite, clicking **Variables** in the Toolbox, and clicking **Make a Variable**. Name the variable after your second group.

    For my project, I created a variable called my broadsheet variable, as shown in Figure 8-15.

Figure 8-15: Preparing the data for the second group of newspapers

15. Copy the scripts shown in Figure 8-16 for the second newspaper sprite.

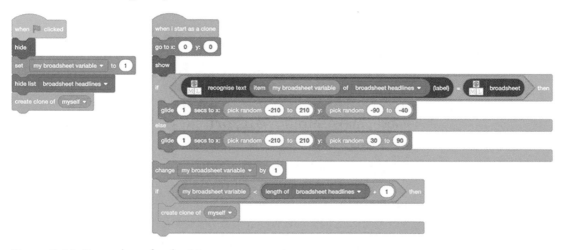

Figure 8-16: Second test for the Newspapers project

These scripts are similar to those you created for the first newspaper sprite in step 9.

This code will go through the examples in your second list. For each one, it will create a sprite, and if your ML model recognizes an example as being in the second group, the code will move it to the bottom half of the screen. Otherwise, the code will move the example to the top half.

Be careful not to use the list or variable from your first sprite. My first script was about the tabloid headlines, and this second script is about the broadsheet headlines.

NOTE *Make sure that your scripts are different and match the sprite they're for.*

Notice that the coordinates also have to be different in this script so that correct matches go to the bottom half of the screen this time.

16. Click the Green Flag again and watch your scripts run.

As before, it's okay if your ML model doesn't get everything right. You can see how my ML model did in Figure 8-17.

How did your ML model perform?

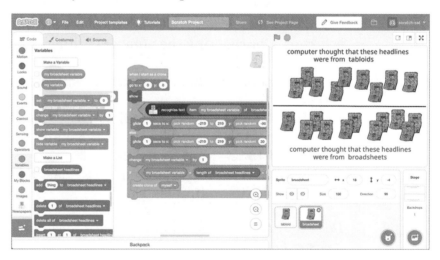

Figure 8-17: Results for the second test of the Newspapers project

REVIEW AND IMPROVE YOUR PROJECT

You've trained an ML model to recognize the use of language in the media! You also used Scratch to make a simple test to visualize how effective your ML model is.

If my ML model had performed perfectly, it would have moved all of the red newspapers to the top half and moved all of the blue newspapers to the bottom half.

It didn't.

Recognizing 100 percent of the headlines correctly was unlikely, as I gave my model only a small amount of training. With more training examples I would expect the results to improve, but even then, ML systems rarely perform perfectly.

But how good was it?

There are many ways that we can describe the performance of an ML system.

MEASURING PERFORMANCE: ACCURACY

One measure we use to describe how well an ML model performs is *accuracy*, or counting the number of things that the ML model answers correctly.

Create a new variable with **for all sprites** selected and call it **correct**.

Change your scripts for the first sprite (the one in Figure 8-12 for newspapers that should go in the top half) to match the scripts in Figure 8-18.

Notice that you'll need to remove the last **if** block in the script to replace it with an **if...else** block.

NOTE *Don't copy the comments in the yellow boxes. I added them to make it easier for you to see which parts of the code are different from the earlier script.*

Now change the scripts for the second sprite (the one in Figure 8-16 for newspapers that should go in the bottom half) to match the scripts in Figure 8-19.

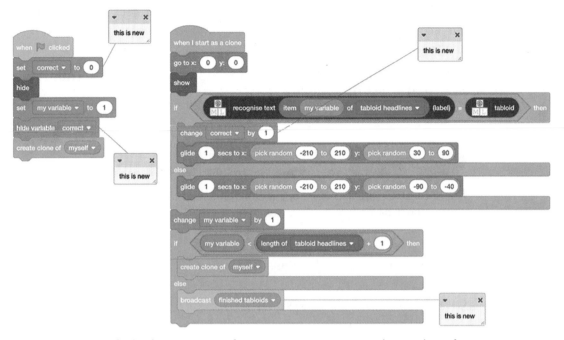

Figure 8-18: Modify the first test script (from Figure 8-12) to count the number of correct answers.

Notice that you'll also need to replace the last **if** block in this script with an **if...else** block.

NOTE *As before, you don't need to copy the comments; they're just there to help you spot the parts that you need to change.*

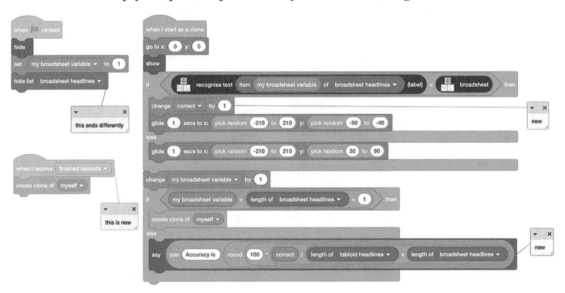

Figure 8-19: Modify the second test script (from Figure 8-16) to count the number of correct answers.

With these updated scripts, your Scratch project will compute the accuracy of your ML model and display the result at the end of the test. The formula is:

correct answers / ((number of tabloid headlines) + (number of broadsheet headlines))

as shown in Figure 8-20.

Figure 8-20: Computing accuracy (Scratch refers to the number of items in a list as the length *of the list)*

In other words, the accuracy is the percentage of how many headlines the ML model classified correctly.

The accuracy for my ML model is shown in Figure 8-21. How does it compare to your project?

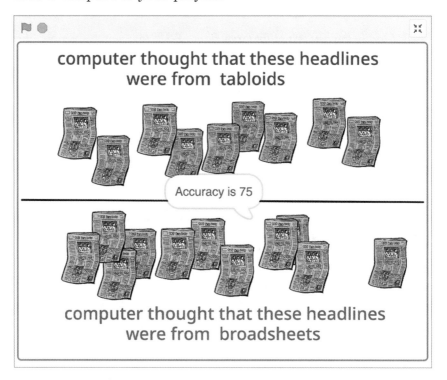

Figure 8-21: Displaying accuracy

MEASURING PERFORMANCE: CONFUSION MATRIX

Accuracy is a useful measure, and possibly the most well-known one. But it's often not enough, so it's normally not the only measure used for real-world ML systems.

Can you think of any problems with accuracy?

What if my ML model thought that everything was a headline from a broadsheet newspaper, as in Figure 8-22?

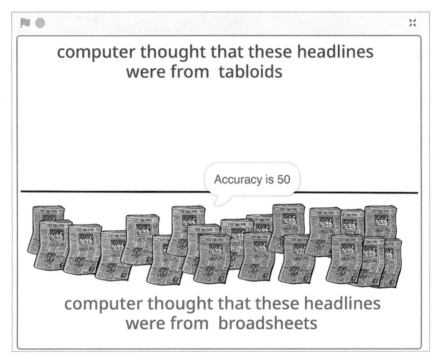

computer thought that these headlines were from tabloids

Accuracy is 50

computer thought that these headlines were from broadsheets

Figure 8-22: Classifying every headline as broadsheet

The accuracy would be 50 percent, as the model would put all 10 broadsheet newspapers in the right place but all 10 tabloid newspapers in the wrong place.

But "50 percent accuracy" isn't a good description of a system that gives the same answer to any question. We need a better way to describe our ML model's performance, one that avoids this sort of misleading result.

A *confusion matrix* is a tool where you count the number of things that the ML model gets correct and the number of things that it gets wrong and then arrange those results in a table. Let's look at an example.

Create four more variables with **for all sprites** selected and name them **true positive**, **true negative**, **false positive**, and **false negative**. Make sure the checkboxes for all four variables are selected in the Toolbox as shown in Figure 8-23.

Figure 8-23: Preparing variables for a confusion matrix

Arrange the variables on the Stage as shown in Figure 8-24.

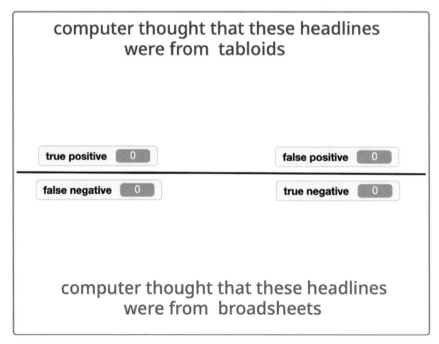

Figure 8-24: Creating a confusion matrix in Scratch

Change your scripts for the first sprite (the one in Figure 8-18 for newspapers that should go in the top half) to match the scripts in Figure 8-25.

It's a bit long, but take your time and compare it carefully to make sure you copy it correctly. As before, I've added comments to highlight the changes.

We're increasing the counters for **true positive** and **false negative**, and changing the **x** values for the glide blocks so that tabloid newspapers stay on the left side of the screen.

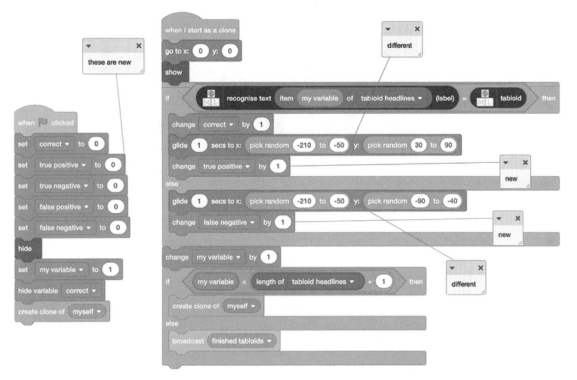

Figure 8-25: Modify the first script (from Figure 8-18) to calculate the confusion matrix values.

Change your scripts for the second sprite (the one in Figure 8-19 for newspapers that should go in the bottom half) to match the scripts in Figure 8-26.

We're increasing the counters for **true negative** and **false positive**, and changing the **x** values for the glide blocks so that broadsheet newspapers stay on the right side of the screen.

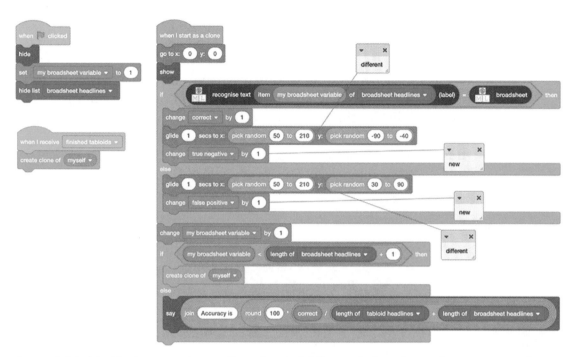

Figure 8-26: Modify the second script (from Figure 8-19) to calculate the confusion matrix values.

Click the Green Flag to test your ML model again. My results are shown in Figure 8-27.

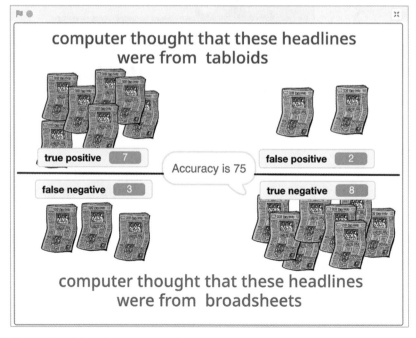

Figure 8-27: Displaying a confusion matrix in Scratch

Table 8-1 shows the results of my ML model arranged in a confusion matrix.

Table 8-1: Arranging Results in a Confusion Matrix

True positive	**False positive**
Headline was from a tabloid. ML model thought it was from a tabloid.	Headline was not from a tabloid. ML model thought it was from a tabloid.
(Correct)	(Incorrect)
False negative	**True negative**
Headline was from a tabloid. ML model thought it was not from a tabloid.	Headline was not from a tabloid. ML model thought it was not from a tabloid.
(Incorrect)	(Correct)

It's a useful way to describe the performance of an ML model that tells us more than accuracy can by itself.

If my ML model thought everything was from a broadsheet newspaper, the confusion matrix would look like Figure 8-28.

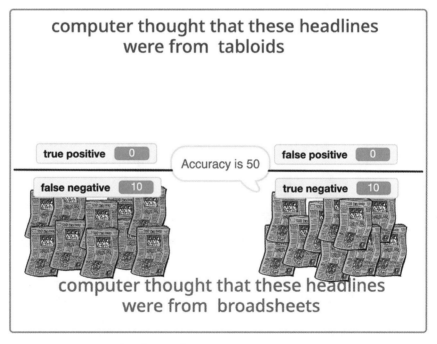

Figure 8-28: Example of a confusion matrix

MEASURING PERFORMANCE: PRECISION AND RECALL

Another way that we describe the performance of ML models is using *precision* and *recall*.

Precision is calculated as **true positive / (true positive + false positive)**.

Recall is calculated as **true positive / (true positive + false negative)**.

You can update your script to include the calculations shown in Figure 8-29. Add them to the end of the **when I start as a clone** script for the second sprite, after the **say** block.

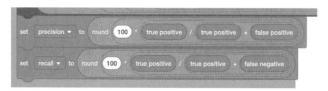

Figure 8-29: Calculating precision and recall in Scratch

I added this calculation to the script for my ML model. Figure 8-30 shows the results I got.

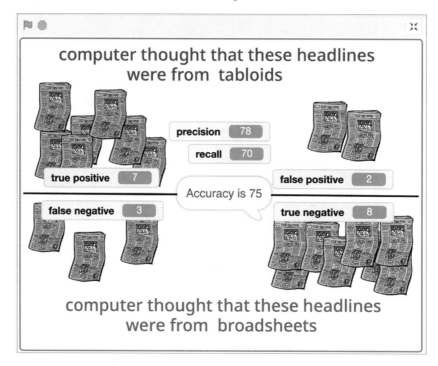

Figure 8-30: Displaying precision and recall in Scratch

The precision score means that when my ML model thinks something is a tabloid headline, it is right 78 percent of the time.

The recall score means that it found 70 percent of the tabloid headlines in the test set.

The accuracy score means that 75 percent of the answers the ML model gave were correct.

Precision, recall, and accuracy all help to give a good description of an ML model's performance.

For example, Figure 8-31 shows results from two different ML models that both have an accuracy score of 50 percent. The other scores help to describe the differences in the way the models are working.

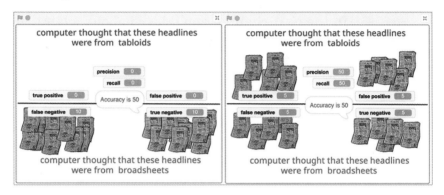

Figure 8-31: Different ML models with 50 percent accuracy

In comparison to the way we tested your project in the last chapter, which was by manually entering test values and getting a feel for how many times the model is correct, using measurement values is a more consistent and effective way to describe the performance of ML models. We'll look at another use of performance measurements for image recognition projects in the next chapter.

IMPROVING YOUR ML MODEL

Try adding another 10 examples to each of your two training buckets from the Train phase and use them to train a new ML model from the Learn & Test phase.

Rerun your Scratch script once the new ML model has finished training.

What does the increased number of training examples do to your precision, recall, and accuracy scores?

WHAT YOU LEARNED

You've seen from all of your own projects that ML isn't perfect and can make mistakes. ML doesn't need to be perfect to be useful, however. ML systems make up for their mistakes by working so quickly, analyzing massive amounts of text that would take a lifetime for a person to read. Even if it makes mistakes 10 percent of the time, an ML system can still be useful at finding things that need attention. But it's important to know how many mistakes an ML system is making to measure how well it is performing.

In this chapter, you learned that there are many ways of testing ML systems and measuring how well they're performing, which can help us decide how to use the results they give us.

In the next chapter, you'll learn about solving more complex problems by breaking them up into separate pieces for an ML model to recognize, and you'll use a confusion matrix again to see how well this works.

9
FINDING AN OBJECT IN A PICTURE

n earlier chapters, you learned that you can train an ML system so that if you give it a picture, it can recognize the object in that picture. That's useful when the whole picture is of something that you're interested in, as it was when you made the Rock, Paper, Scissors game in Chapter 4. For that game, your hand filled the photo. But sometimes we want the computer to learn to find something that's only a small part of a much bigger picture. In this chapter, you'll see how to break up a complex job into separate simpler parts and then use ML for each part.

For example, imagine that you want to use ML to find where the tree is in Figure 9-1.

Figure 9-1: Where is the tree?

The basic idea is that you train an ML model to recognize pictures of trees, in the same way that you trained it to recognize pictures of certain animals in Chapter 3. Then, you chop up this new photo into smaller pieces and use that ML model to check which piece looks like a picture of a tree.

For example, the top-left piece of Figure 9-1 is shown in Figure 9-2. The ML model wouldn't recognize this picture as a tree, so we can say that the tree isn't in the top left of the picture.

Figure 9-2: Top left of Figure 9-1

Or, we could try the bottom-right piece shown in Figure 9-3. The ML model wouldn't recognize this picture as a tree either, so we can say that the tree isn't in the bottom right of the picture.

Figure 9-3: Bottom right of Figure 9-1

We keep going until we try testing a picture like Figure 9-4. When we get a piece that the ML model has high confidence looks like a picture of a tree, we know that we've found the location of the tree.

Figure 9-4: Bottom left of Figure 9-1

A good way to think of it is that you're breaking the picture up into tiles and testing each tile separately. In this chapter, you'll see for yourself how this method works as you train an ML model to find where something is in randomly generated scenes.

BUILD YOUR PROJECT

For this chapter, we'll use a Scratch project that chooses a random backdrop and then randomly distributes a dozen sprites around the Stage. One of the sprites is a duck. The aim of this project is to find the duck only by looking at the Stage, without cheating by using the coordinates of the sprite (see Figure 9-5).

Figure 9-5: The objective of this project is to find the duck.

TRAIN YOUR MODEL

1. Create a new ML project, name it **Find the duck**, and set it to learn to recognize images.

NOTE *If you're not sure how to create an ML project, read the section "Creating a New ML Project" on page 9 in Chapter 2.*

2. Click **Train**, as shown in Figure 9-6.

Figure 9-6: Train is the first phase of an ML project.

3. Click **Add new label**, as shown in Figure 9-7. Then enter **Duck**.

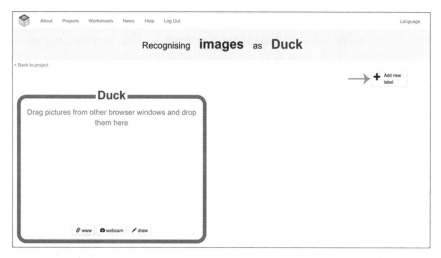

Figure 9-7: Create a training bucket for examples of duck pictures.

4. Click **Add new label** again and name this bucket **Not the Duck**, as shown in Figure 9-8. (The underscores will be added automatically.)

   This bucket will be used to store *negative training examples*, which are examples of things that *aren't* what you want the computer to learn to recognize.

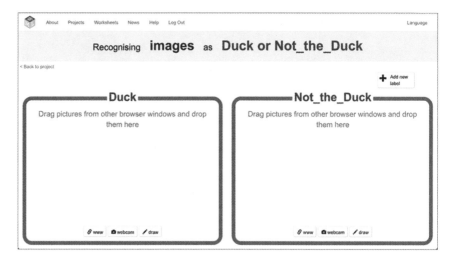

Figure 9-8: Create a training bucket for examples of pictures not of the duck.

5. Click **Back to project** in the top-left corner of the screen.
6. Click **Make**.
7. Click **Scratch 3**, as shown in Figure 9-9.

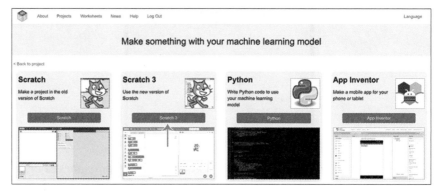

Figure 9-9: Click **Scratch 3**.

You'll see a warning that you don't have an ML model yet. That's fine, as you'll be using Scratch to collect the training examples.

8. Click **straight into Scratch**, as shown in Figure 9-10.

*Figure 9-10: Open Scratch without an ML model by clicking **straight into Scratch**.*

9. Click **Project templates** in the top menu. Then click **Find the duck** in the list of templates displayed.

   The project has 12 sprites arranged on the Stage into a 3×4 grid of tiles. The sprites are hidden when you first load the template, but they're named as shown in Figure 9-11.

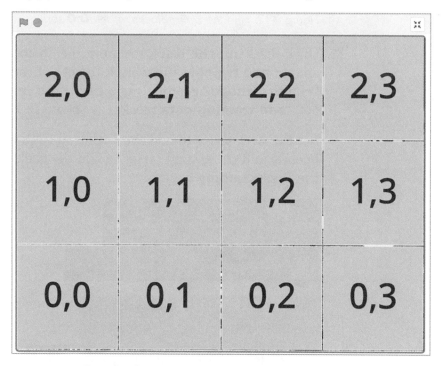

Figure 9-11: The sprites in the Find the duck template.

10. Click the **0,0** sprite in the sprites list at the bottom right. At the top left of the Code Area, under the yellow TRAINING comment, find the **store training data example of the duck** and the **store training data example of NOT the duck** blocks, as shown in Figure 9-12.

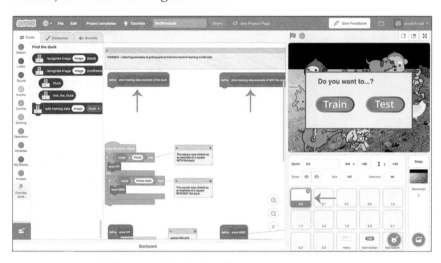

Figure 9-12: Find the script blocks for the **0,0** sprite.

11. Click the **Find the duck** group in the Toolbox on the left, and add an **add training data** block to both of the scripts. Then, from the **Images** group, drag a **backdrop image** block into both **add training data** blocks, as shown in Figure 9-13.

Set the first script to add the backdrop to the Duck training bucket, and the second script to add the backdrop to the Not the Duck training bucket.

Figure 9-13: Add training examples to the two training buckets.

12. Repeat step 11 for all 12 sprites (see Figure 9-14). Once you've done that, any of the tiles you click can be used to add an example to your training data.

NOTE *If a block glows yellow while you're adding blocks to it, you accidentally ran that part of the script, which adds pictures to your training buckets. If that happens, go back to the Train phase and delete those pictures from the buckets.*

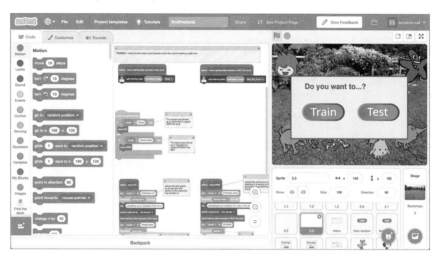

Figure 9-14: Add the script blocks to all 12 sprites.

13. It's time to collect your training examples! Click the Green Flag to start. When the project asks if you want to Train or Test, click **Train**.

    Click **OK** when you're asked to click the duck, and then click the tile with the duck in it. The tile you click will be added to your Duck training bucket, as shown in Figure 9-15.

NOTE *The whole duck probably won't fit neatly into one tile, so you might only see part of it. That's still useful for testing, as you'll soon see.*

14. Click **OK** when you're asked to click a tile that doesn't have the duck in it. Make sure to click a tile that doesn't show *any* part of the duck.

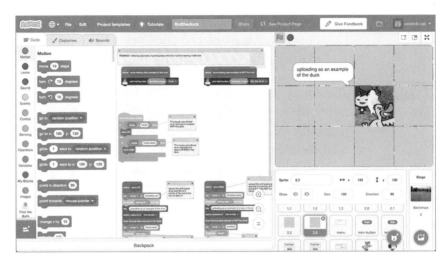

Figure 9-15: Adding an example of the duck to the training data

15. On the Machine Learning for Kids site, click **Back to project** and then click **Train** to make sure that everything is working. You should see both of the tiles you clicked, as shown in Figure 9-16. Check that they're in the correct buckets.

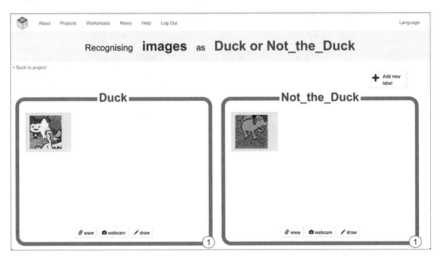

Figure 9-16: Training examples should show up in the correct buckets back in the Train phase.

NOTE *If either tile is missing, you might have missed adding the **add training data** blocks to one of the sprite scripts, so click each sprite in the sprites list to double-check.*

16. Repeat steps 13 through 15 in Scratch until you've got 10 examples in each bucket, as shown in Figure 9-17.

    Here are two tips for your **Not the Duck** training examples:

    ▸ Make sure you don't click the same character every time for your **Not the Duck** bucket. You don't want that to become a training set for recognizing the parrot, for example. The best way to make a good **Not the Duck** training set is to click an even mix of the other characters.

    ▸ Second, try to include some tiles with no characters at all. You want the computer to learn that empty tiles are also *not the duck.*

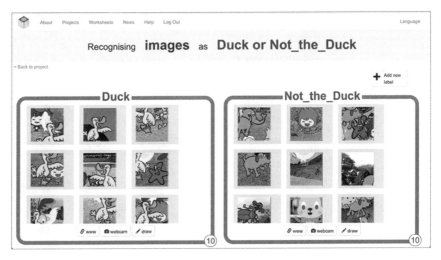

Figure 9-17: Training data for finding the duck

17. Click **Back to project** and then **Learn & Test**. Click **Train new machine learning model**, as shown in Figure 9-18.

    Wait for the model to finish training. This might take a few minutes.

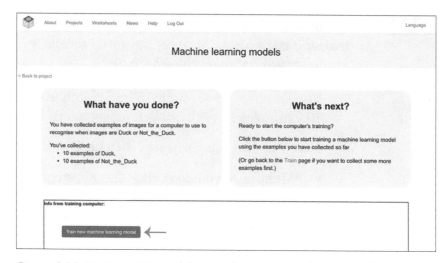

Figure 9-18: Train an ML model using the examples that you collected.

PREPARE YOUR PROJECT

Next, you need to modify your Scratch project to finish the test scripts.

1. Click the **0,0** sprite in the sprites list at the bottom right and find the **when I receive test-0,0** script in the Code Area. It's to the right of the scripts you worked on before, as shown in Figure 9-19.

Figure 9-19: Find the test script in the **0,0** sprite.

2. In the **when I receive test-0,0** script, drag in a **recognise image (label)** block from the **Find the duck** group and update it as shown in Figure 9-20.

This script will use your ML model to test whether the bottom-left tile contains the duck and display the message "Is the duck here?" if it does.

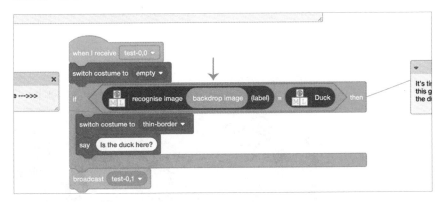

Figure 9-20: Update the test script to use your ML model.

3. Repeat step 2 for all 12 sprites (see Figure 9-21). Once you've done this, your ML model can check all of the tiles to look for the duck.

Figure 9-21: Add the test blocks to all 12 sprites.

TEST YOUR PROJECT

It's time to test your ML model!

1. Click the Green Flag and then click **Test** in the Scratch project on the Stage.

    Your project will use your ML model to test every tile and highlight any it recognizes as the duck, as shown in Figure 9-22.

Figure 9-22: Testing your ML model

2. Try it a few times and see how often your model gets it right. Finding a small image inside of a large scene is a complex job, so with only 10 training examples, it will probably make a few mistakes.

3. Add another 10 training examples to each bucket by clicking the Green Flag and clicking **Train** as you did earlier. You can check your new training examples back in the Train phase, as shown in Figure 9-23.

Click **Back to project** and then **Learn & Test** to train a new ML model with your larger set of training examples.

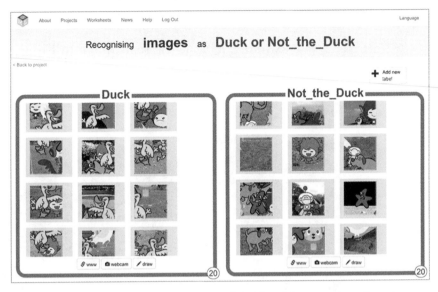

Figure 9-23: Try training a new ML model using 20 examples of each group.

4. Test again as you did before. Is your new ML model better at finding the duck?

REVIEW AND IMPROVE YOUR PROJECT

How can you describe how well the ML model is doing?

In Chapter 8, you learned that you can keep a count of the number of times the computer gets things right and wrong:

True positive Tiles the computer thought included the duck, and did

False positive Tiles the computer thought included the duck, but didn't

True negative Tiles the computer thought didn't include the duck, and didn't

False negative Tiles the computer thought didn't include the duck, but did

You can use this count to draw up a confusion matrix and calculate the accuracy, recall, and precision of your ML model.

NOTE *If you don't remember how to calculate these numbers or make a confusion matrix, see the section "Review and Improve Your Project" on page 118 in Chapter 8.*

For example, look at the test image in Figure 9-24.

Figure 9-24: A test image with the two bottom-right tiles recognized as a match

The duck was present in the four tiles in the bottom right of the board. Two of them were recognized by my ML model. Two were missed. So, my confusion matrix looks like this:

True positives	False positives
2	0
False negatives	**True negatives**
2	8

This confusion matrix gives me:

Precision: 100%

(Every time my ML model thought it saw a duck, there was a duck there.)

Recall: 50%

(My ML model found half of the tiles that contained a duck.)

Accuracy: 83%

(My ML model gave 10 correct answers out of 12 total answers.)

You need a larger sample size, including several different backgrounds, to really trust these numbers.

I ran this test five times, and my overall results were as follows:

True positives	False positives
9	0
False negatives	**True negatives**
6	45

Precision: 100%

Recall: 60%

Accuracy: 90%

These numbers give us a more meaningful way of describing the performance of the ML model.

My model, which was trained with only a small number of examples, seems to be very precise (when it recognizes a duck, it is always correct). However, it misses things sometimes.

We describe a precise model that sometimes misses things as *favoring precision over recall*. This is a good approach for projects where it is important not to falsely recognize things.

For projects where it is more important to not miss anything, and where it is okay to make the occasional mistake, you would aim to train ML models in a way that *favors recall over precision* instead.

How is your project performing?

REAL-WORLD APPLICATIONS FOR COMPLEX IMAGE RECOGNITION SYSTEMS

You might have trained an image recognition ML model like this before. Have you ever been asked by a website to prove that you're a human by clicking pictures of street signs as in Figure 9-25? Or bicycles? Or taxis?

Figure 9-25: Helping to train an ML model

Hopefully you can see how this kind of image recognition application, known as a *CAPTCHA*, would be a great way to collect a large number of training examples for an image recognition system that can find different things on the street. Do you think this would be useful in the development of self-driving cars?

The basic idea here is described in the chapter's introduction. If we want to find something small in a larger picture, we chop the picture up into smaller tiles and test each tile individually with an ML model trained to recognize pictures of that object.

You probably have a feel for the sorts of challenges of this technique from training it yourself. For example, one of the biggest problems is deciding what size tiles to use. Remember the example of finding the tree in Figure 9-1?

If you make your tiles too small, you might only ever see a small section of the object you're trying to find and never recognize it. For example, your ML model might not recognize Figure 9-26 as a tree.

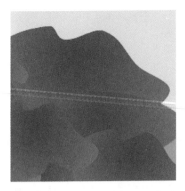

Figure 9-26: A tile that includes only part of the tree

On the other hand, if you make your tiles too big, as in Figure 9-27, you still have the problem of there being too much in the picture that *isn't* the tree, which will challenge an ML model trained to recognize pictures of trees.

Figure 9-27: A tile that is too large to focus on the tree

If you know the likely size of the object you're looking for in the picture, you can make a sensible estimate for the right tile size to use. Some systems even ask users to specify the tile size to use.

If neither of these solutions is an option, you can try a wide variety of tile sizes and use the result that gives your model the highest confidence, as shown in Figure 9-28.

Even if you get the grid size right, the object you're looking for won't always fit neatly in the middle of a tile (as you probably noticed with the duck).

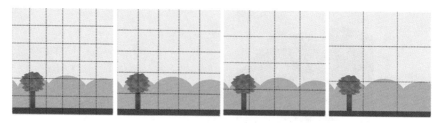

Figure 9-28: Try a variety of tile sizes if you have no way to know the best size.

To improve your chance of finding a tile with the object you want in the middle, you also need to try different starting positions.

Systems that use a combination of these techniques can be very effective. For example, in 2015, during a state of emergency caused by a drought in California, an ML model was used to find lawns, swimming pools, and other features that affect water usage.

Cutting the satellite images for the whole state into tiles, just as you've done in your project, meant each tile could be individually classified. The main difference was that the California ML model was trained to recognize not just one thing, but several different things, that impact water usage. (You saw in Chapter 3 how you can train an ML model to recognize pictures of different objects.) Combining image recognition with a map meant California officials could quickly understand the impact of water usage across the state.

California is a huge state, and to manually perform such a census or survey would have taken a long time. ML was a fast and efficient way to come up with a useful estimate, and in times of emergency, speed and efficiency are very important.

ML image recognition techniques are also regularly used in businesses. For example, drones can take high-resolution photos while flying over buildings, roofs, bridges, solar panels, pipes, and much more. These photos are then chopped into tiles and tested by an ML model trained to recognize signs of damage or poor maintenance and repair. Automated image recognition systems based on the same principles as this chapter's project are used in a variety of fields, such as civil engineering (for inspecting bridges and buildings), agriculture (for recognizing healthy or diseased plants and crops), or even public safety (such as in Australia, where ML is used in lifesaver drones that can recognize sharks from the air).

WHAT YOU LEARNED

In this chapter, you trained an ML model to recognize objects that are part of a larger scene. This is the most complicated project you've done so far, but hopefully you now have a good understanding of how complex image recognition systems are built. You learned some of the challenges of training such systems, like knowing how to break up the complex task into simpler tasks (such as by choosing the correct tile size), and you got some tips for solving them. You also saw some real-world applications for these kinds of complex ML systems and examples of the fields where they're used.

In the next chapter, we'll look at another common use of ML: smart assistants.

10
SMART ASSISTANTS

n this chapter, we'll look at a common household use of ML: smart assistants like Siri, Alexa, or Google Home that can do simple jobs for you when you ask, like set an alarm, start a timer, or play some music.

Smart assistants are ML systems trained to recognize the meaning of text. You've seen that you can train a computer so that when you give it some writing, the computer can recognize what you're trying to say. And if a computer can understand what you mean, it can understand what you're asking it to do.

To create a program that categorizes text based on recognizing the text's intention (*intent classification*), we collect a large number of examples of each type of command that we want it to recognize and then use ML to train a model.

From the projects you've done so far, you're already familiar with the *classification* part of intent classification. For example, messages can be classified as compliments or insults, and newspaper headlines can be classified as tabloids or broadsheets. The computer knows about some categories of writing, and when you give it some text, it tries to *classify* that text, or work out which category that text should go into. The *intent* part is because we're using the ability to classify the text to recognize its intention.

Intent classification is useful for building computer systems that we can interact with in a natural way. For example, a computer could recognize that when you say, "Turn on the light," the intention is for a light to be switched on. This is described as a *natural language interface*. In other words, instead of needing to press a switch to turn the light on, you're using *natural language*—a language that has evolved naturally in humans, not one designed for computers—to communicate that intent.

The computer learns from the patterns in the examples we give it—patterns in the words we choose, the way we phrase commands, how we combine words for certain types of commands, and when we use commands that are short versus longer, just to name a few.

In this chapter, you'll make a virtual smart assistant that can recognize your commands and carry out your instructions (see Figure 10-1).

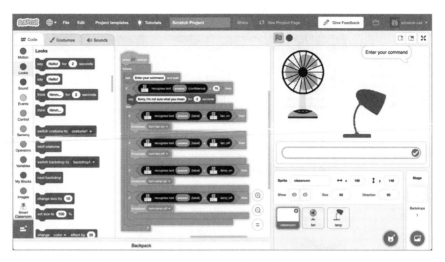

Figure 10-1: Making a smart assistant in Scratch

Let's get started!

BUILD YOUR PROJECT

To start with, you'll train the ML model to recognize commands to turn two devices—a fan and a lamp—on or off.

CODE YOUR PROJECT WITHOUT ML

As we saw in Chapter 7, it's useful to see the difference that ML makes by trying to code an AI project without it first. You can skip this step if you feel you have a good grasp of the difference between a rule-based approach and ML and would rather go straight to using ML.

1. Go to Scratch at *https://machinelearningforkids.co.uk/scratch3/*.
2. Click **Project templates** at the top of the screen, as shown in Figure 10-2.

Figure 10-2: Project templates include starter projects to save you time.

3. Click the **Smart Classroom** template.

4. Copy the script shown in Figure 10-3.

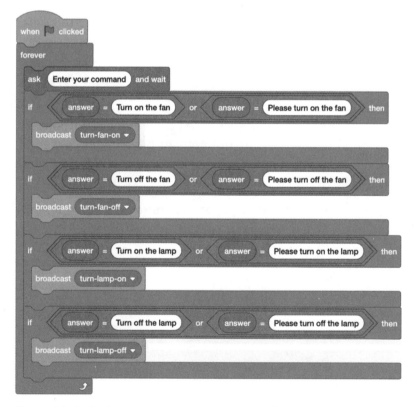

Figure 10-3: Coding a smart assistant using rules

This script asks you to enter a command. If you type Turn on (or off) the fan (or lamp), Scratch will play the corresponding animation. Let's try it out.

5. Test your project by clicking the Green Flag. Type the command **Turn on the fan** and check that the fan really does start spinning.

    What happens if you spell something wrong? What happens if you change the wording (for example, "Turn on the fan please")? What happens if you don't mention the word *fan* (for example, "I'm very hot, we need some air in here!")?

    Why don't these work?

    Do you think it's possible to write a script that would work with any phrasing of these four commands?

    Think back to the definition in Chapter 1, where I said ML is not the only way to create AI systems. Here you've created an AI project using a rules-based approach instead of ML. By trying other techniques like this one and seeing where they fall short, you can better understand why ML is preferred for so many projects.

TRAIN YOUR MODEL

1. Create a new ML project, name it **Smart Classroom**, and set it to learn to recognize text in your preferred language.

NOTE   *If you're not sure how to create an ML project, read the section "Creating a New ML Project" on page 9 in Chapter 2.*

2. Click **Train**, as shown in Figure 10-4.

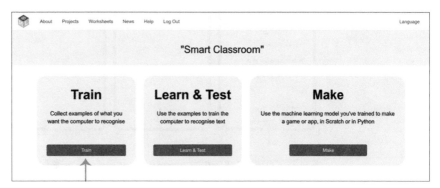

Figure 10-4: The first phase is to collect training examples.

3. Click **Add new label**, as shown in Figure 10-5, and create a training bucket called **fan on**. Repeat this step to create three more training buckets named **fan off**, **lamp on**, and **lamp off**. (The underscores will be added automatically.)

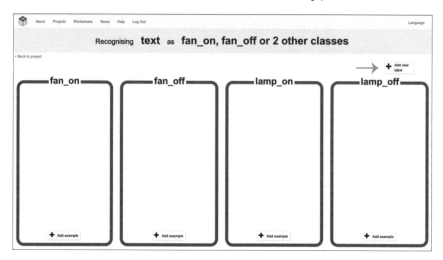

Figure 10-5: Create training buckets for the commands to recognize.

4. Click **Add example** in the **fan_on** bucket and type an example of how you would ask someone to turn on the fan, as shown in Figure 10-6.

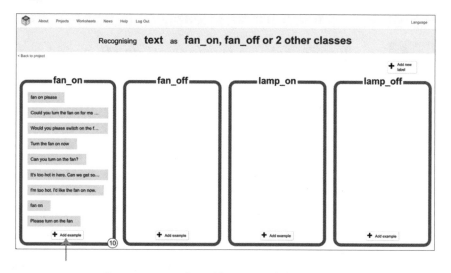

Figure 10-6: Collecting examples of how to ask for the fan to be turned on

It can be short (for example, "fan on please") or long ("Could you turn the fan on for me now, please?").

It can be polite ("Would you please switch on the fan?") or less polite ("Turn the fan on now").

It can include the words *fan* and *on* ("Can you turn on the fan?") or neither ("It's too hot in here. Can we get some air in here, please?").

Type as many as you can think of, as shown in Figure 10-6. You need at least five examples, but I've given you six already, so that should be easy!

5. Click **Add example** in the **fan_off** bucket, as shown in Figure 10-7.

    This time, type as many examples as you can think of for asking someone to turn off the fan. You need at least five examples. These are the examples your ML model will use to learn what a "fan off" command looks like.

    Try to include some examples that don't include the words *fan* or *off*.

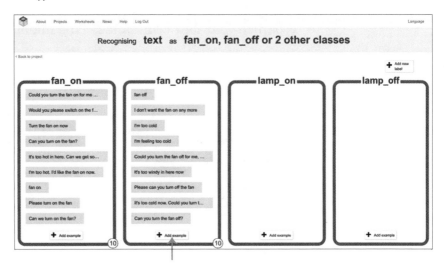

Figure 10-7: Collecting examples of how to ask for the fan to be turned off

6. Repeat this process for the last two buckets, until you have at least five examples for all four commands, as shown in Figure 10-8.

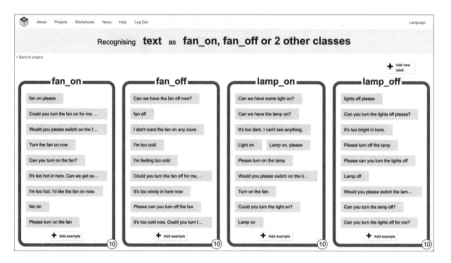

Figure 10-8: Training data for the smart assistant project

7. Click **Back to project** in the top-left corner of the screen.

8. Click **Learn & Test**.

9. Click **Train new machine learning model**, as shown in Figure 10-9.

    The computer will use the examples you've written to learn how to recognize your four commands. This might take a minute.

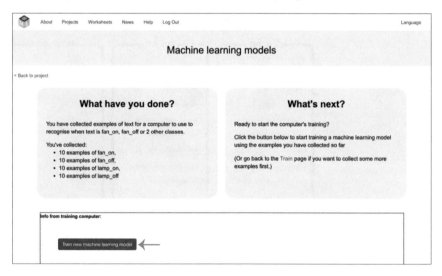

Figure 10-9: Train an ML model for your smart assistant.

10. After training an ML model, we test it to see how good it is at recognizing new commands. Type a command into the **Test** box, as shown in Figure 10-10.

Make sure you test the model with commands that you didn't include in the training buckets. You're not interested in whether the computer can remember what you've already told it, but in whether it can recognize commands it hasn't seen before.

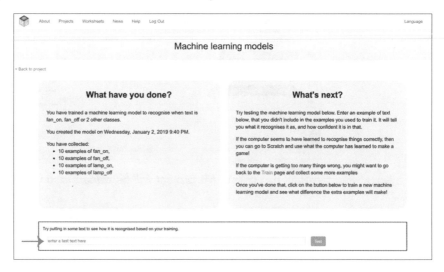

Figure 10-10: Testing your ML model

If the model makes mistakes, you can go back to the Train phase and add more examples of the commands that it keeps getting wrong. This is like a teacher using a student's poor exam result to figure out which subjects they need to review with the student to help improve the student's understanding.

Once you've added more examples, go back to the Learn & Test phase and train a new ML model. Then test it again to see if the computer is any better at recognizing commands.

CODE YOUR PROJECT WITH ML

Now that you have an ML model that is able to recognize your commands, you can re-create the earlier project to use ML instead of the rules you used before.

1. Click **Back to project** in the top-left corner of the screen.
2. Click **Make**.
3. Click **Scratch 3**, and then click **Open in Scratch 3** to open a new window in Scratch.

    You should see a new set of blocks for your ML project in the Toolbox, as shown in Figure 10-11.

Figure 10-11: Your ML project will be added to the Scratch Toolbox.

4. Click **Project templates** in the top menu bar and choose the **Smart Classroom** template.

5. Copy the script shown in Figure 10-12.

   When you give this script commands, it will use your ML model to recognize the command and carry out the instruction.

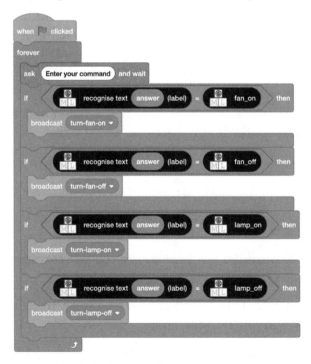

Figure 10-12: ML approach for a smart assistant

TEST YOUR PROJECT

Test your project by clicking the Green Flag and entering a variety of commands, phrased in lots of different ways. See how your smart assistant performs now compared to the version that didn't use ML.

REVIEW AND IMPROVE YOUR PROJECT

You've created your own smart assistant: a virtual version of Amazon's Alexa or Apple's Siri that can understand and carry out your commands! What could you do to improve the way that it behaves?

USING YOUR MODEL'S CONFIDENCE SCORE

Back in the Learn & Test phase, you should have noticed the confidence score displayed when you tested your model. That tells you how confident the computer is that it has recognized a command.

Go back to the Learn & Test phase now and try typing something that doesn't fit into one of the four commands that the computer has learned to recognize.

For example, you could try "What is the capital city of France?" as shown in Figure 10-13.

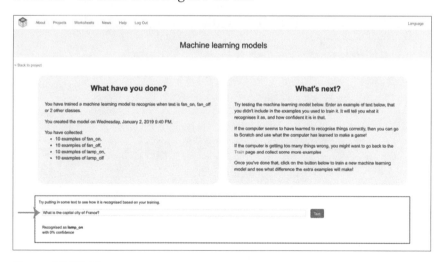

Figure 10-13: Testing your smart assistant

My ML model recognized it as "lamp on," but it had 0 percent confidence in that classification. That was the ML model's way of telling me that it hadn't recognized the command.

"What is the capital city of France?" doesn't look like any of the examples I've given the ML model. The question doesn't match the patterns it has identified in the examples I used to train it. This means it can't confidently recognize the question as one of the four commands it's been trained to recognize.

Your ML model might have a higher confidence than 0, but it should still be a relatively low number. (If not, try adding more examples to train your ML model with.)

Experiment with other questions and commands that don't have anything to do with a fan or lamp. Compare the confidence scores your ML model gives with those it displays when it recognizes actual fan on, fan off, lamp on, and lamp off commands. What kinds of confidence scores does your ML model give when it's correctly recognized something?

Once you have a feel for how the confidence scores work for your ML model, you can use that in your Scratch project. Update your script to look like Figure 10-14.

Now, if the model isn't at least 80 percent confident that it has understood the command correctly, it will display a "sorry" response for 2 seconds and not carry out the action.

You'll need to change the **80** value in this script to a percentage that matches the behavior of your own ML model.

What else could you do to improve your project?

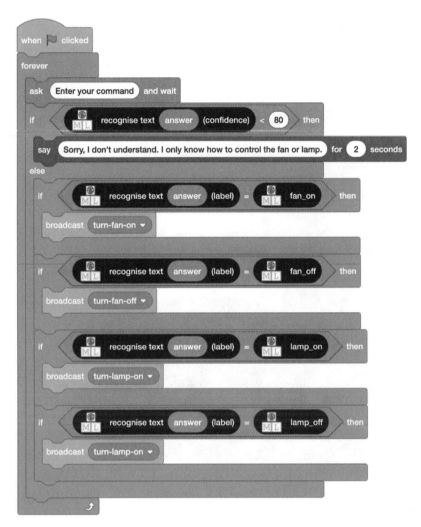

Figure 10-14: Using confidence scores in your ML project

USING SPEECH INPUT INSTEAD OF TYPING

You could modify your project to be more like real-world smart assistants by using voice input instead of typing.

In the Toolbox, click the Extensions Library icon (it looks like two blocks and a plus sign), add the **Speech to Text** extension, and update your script as shown in Figure 10-5.

At the time of writing, the Scratch Speech to Text extension can be used only in the Google Chrome web browser.

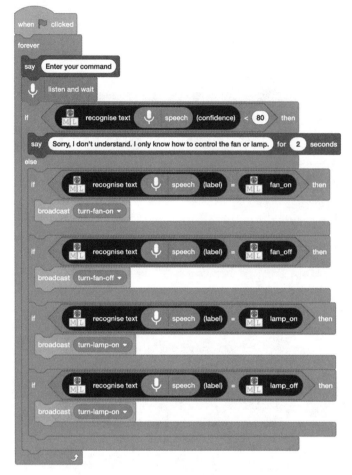

Figure 10-15: Adding speech recognition to your smart assistant

What else could you do to improve your project?

COLLECTING TRAINING DATA

ML is often used for recognizing text because it's quicker than having to write rules. But training a model properly requires lots and lots of examples. To build these systems in the real world, we'd need more efficient ways of collecting examples than simply typing them all yourself like you've done so far. For example, instead of asking one person to write 100 examples, it might be better to ask 100 people to write one example each. Or 1,000 people. Or 10,000 people.

If you can figure out when your ML model gets something wrong, you can collect more examples to add to your training buckets. For example, what if the ML model has a very low confidence score? Or what if someone keeps giving a similar command in slightly different ways? That probably means that the ML model isn't recognizing the commands correctly or doing what the person wants, and that's helpful feedback for your training. What if the person clicks a thumbs-down "I'm not happy" button? What if they end up pressing a button to do something? What if they sound more and more annoyed?

There are lots of ways to guess that something hasn't worked well. And every time that happens, that's an example you could collect and add to one of your training buckets so a newer ML model can work a little better next time.

We use all these sorts of techniques (collecting training examples from large numbers of people, getting feedback from users, and many more) to help us build computers and devices that can understand what you mean.

WHAT YOU LEARNED

In this chapter, we've looked at how ML is used to recognize the meaning of text, and how it can be used to build computer systems that can understand what we mean and do what we ask.

In your project, you used the same type of ML technology that enables *smart assistants* like Amazon's Alexa, Google Home, Microsoft's Cortana, and Apple's Siri. *Natural language interfaces* let us tell our devices what we want them to do by using languages like English, instead of only by pressing screens or buttons.

When you ask a smartphone what the time is, or to set an alarm or a timer, or to play your favorite song, the computer needs to classify that command. It needs to take that series of words that you chose and recognize their intent.

The makers of smartphones and smart assistants trained an ML model to recognize the meaning of user commands by working out a list of categories—all of the possible commands they thought users might want to give. And then for each one, they collected lots and lots of examples of how someone might give that command.

In both this project and the real world, the process works like this:

1. Predict commands that you might give.
2. Collect examples of each of those commands.
3. Use those examples to train an ML model.
4. Script or code what you want the computer to do when it recognizes each command.

To create a real smart assistant, you'd have to repeat these steps for thousands of commands, not just four. And you would need thousands, or tens of thousands, of examples for each command.

In the next chapter, you'll use this capability to build programs that can answer questions.

11
CHATBOTS

n the last chapter, we talked about *intent classification*: building ML systems that can recognize the meaning (the intention) of text. We talked about one common use of intent classification, which is to build smart assistants that can understand what we're telling them and carry out our commands.

In this chapter, we'll look at how ML models that understand the meaning of text can be used to build *question answering (QA) systems*. QA systems recognize and respond to our questions, discovering the answers automatically from a set of documents.

Unlike search engines, which return a list of web pages, QA systems return a specific answer to a specific question. This is more challenging, as it requires a deep understanding of both the question and the meaning of the web pages or documents that may contain the answers. For example, the correct answer to a question like "Who was President Cleveland's wife?" is "Frances Folsom," not a list of documents that include biographies of US presidents.

QA has been a goal and active area of AI research for many years. For example, the US National Institute of Standards and Technology (NIST) has run a QA competition every year since 1999, where universities and companies compete to see which of their computer systems can answer the most questions correctly.

Perhaps better known is the IBM QA computer system Watson, which, as mentioned in Chapter 1, competed on the US television quiz show *Jeopardy!* and beat two champions. *Jeopardy!* is known for asking complex and sometimes tricky questions on a huge variety of topics, and therefore is a particularly challenging test for a computer.

Chatbots, programs that imitate human conversation, are a simpler task for computers than QA systems, for many reasons. First, a chatbot is generally created to answer questions about a single fairly small and specific topic, whereas QA systems attempt to answer questions on any topic.

In addition, chatbot responses are often prepared in advance. Simple chatbots usually aren't expected to be able to find the answer for themselves. Complex chatbots may have more detailed scripts that allow for follow-up or clarifying questions, but the general principle is the same.

Chatbots are becoming very common. They're often used for customer service, where companies need to answer questions from the public about their products and services. Frequently asked questions can be quickly and efficiently answered, with more complex questions quickly redirected to human customer service representatives.

You can find chatbots and virtual assistants on many websites and phone apps—taking your pizza order, recommending clothing and fashion accessories, answering questions about the weather, managing your bank account, arranging meetings and appointments, finding a restaurant and booking a table, offering advice to help you manage a medical condition, and much more.

In this project, you'll create your own chatbot and train it to answer questions on a topic of your choice (as shown in Figure 11-1). We'll follow this process:

1. Predict questions that users might ask.
2. Collect examples of how to ask each of those questions.
3. Use those examples to train an ML model.
4. Prepare the answer the computer should give when it recognizes each question.

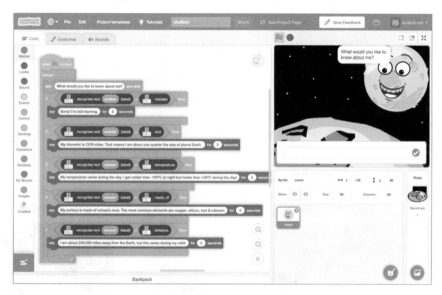

Figure 11-1: Chatbots use ML to answer our questions.

Let's get started!

BUILD YOUR PROJECT

Decide what you'd like your chatbot to answer questions about. This can be any topic you like, but here are a few suggestions to help if you can't think of one:

▶   Your favorite book
▶   Your favorite TV show

- Your favorite sports team
- Your favorite actor, author, or music artist
- Space, planets, and the solar system
- Dinosaurs
- A period of history, such as ancient Rome or the Viking Age

For the screenshots in this chapter, I made a chatbot that answers questions about the moon.

PREPARE YOUR CHARACTER

Go to Scratch at *https://machinelearningforkids.co.uk/scratch3/* and add a backdrop and a character for your QA chatbot.

Make sure the scene you create matches your topic. For example, if you're making a chatbot to answer questions about the Roman Empire, you could draw a Roman centurion in a battlefield.

For my chatbot about the moon, I drew a space-themed backdrop, as shown in Figure 11-2.

NOTE   *For a refresher on creating a backdrop, see step 6 on page 28 in Chapter 3. For a review of creating a sprite, see step 9 on page 59 in Chapter 5.*

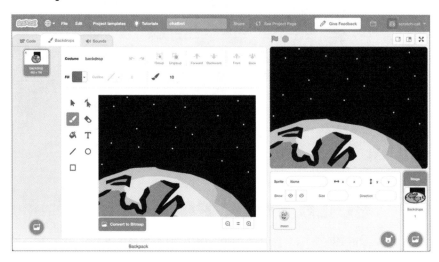

Figure 11-2: Create a custom backdrop for your chatbot character.

For my chatbot character, I made a moon sprite and added cartoon eyes and a mouth, as shown in Figure 11-3.

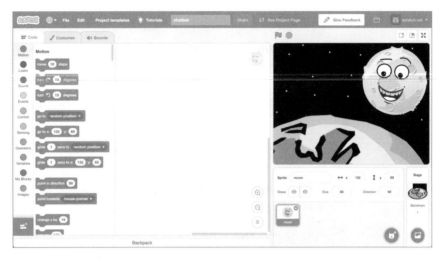

Figure 11-3: Create a custom sprite for your chatbot character.

If you'd prefer not to draw, you can click Choose a Backdrop or Choose a Sprite to select a premade option. Or, you can click Upload a Sprite or Upload a Backdrop to use pictures you've saved from the internet. For example, if you're making a chatbot about your favorite band, you could use a photo of them. If you're making a chatbot about a school or company, you could use its logo.

Once you've created your chatbot scene, make sure you save your Scratch project, as you'll need it later. If you're not sure how to do that, read the section "Saving Your Work" on page xxiv in the introduction.

TRAIN YOUR MODEL

1. Create a new ML project, name it **Chatbot**, and set it to learn to recognize text in your preferred language.

NOTE *If you're not sure how to create an ML project, read the section "Creating a New ML Project" on page 9 in Chapter 2.*

2. Click **Train**, as shown in Figure 11-4.

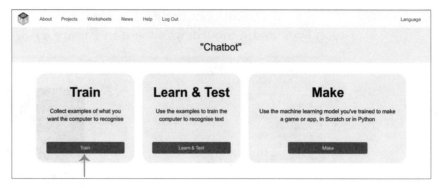

Figure 11-4: Train is the first phase of an ML project.

3. Think of the most common question people might ask about your chosen topic.

    For my topic, the moon, I'm guessing that people will ask how big the moon is.

    When you've chosen your first question, click **Add new label**, as shown in Figure 11-5, and type in a word or two that represents that question. For example, I used size for my training bucket label.

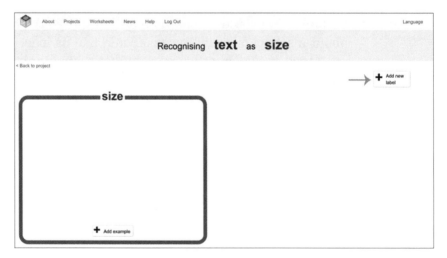

Figure 11-5: Create a bucket to represent examples of your first question.

4. Click **Add example** and enter a way to ask that question, as shown in Figure 11-6.

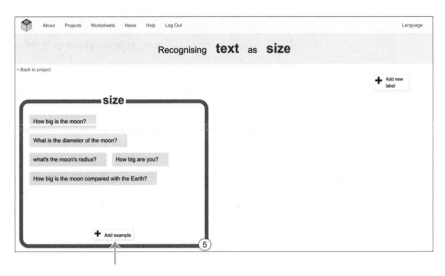

Figure 11-6: Add examples of different ways to ask the first question.

Think of how different people might phrase the question when they ask it. You don't need to worry about the answer for now.

Type in as many ways of asking this question as you can think of, making sure you have at least five examples. These examples will be used to train an ML model to recognize when someone is asking this question.

If your chatbot looks like the topic you're asking questions about (like my cartoon moon answering questions about the moon), then you could include some example questions directed to the character, such as "How big are you?".

5. Think of more types of questions about your topic. Click **Add new label** again to create a training bucket for each type of question, and **Add example** to add examples of how to ask that question. As before, you need at least five examples for each type of question.

For my project, I started with four types of questions, with five examples for each (see Figure 11-7). Your project will vary depending on your topic and the number of questions you can think of for it.

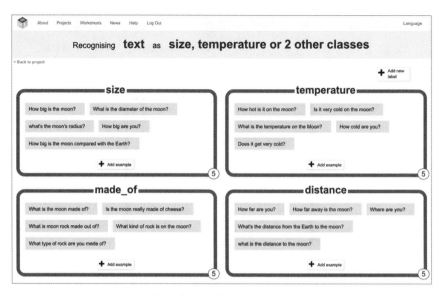

Figure 11-7: Write examples of the different types of questions someone could ask.

For your topic, you're guessing what the most common questions are and imagining the different ways that people might ask them. Real-world ML projects often collect these examples from actual customers or users so that the computer can learn what questions are really being asked, and how. For example, a shop training a virtual assistant to answer questions about setting up televisions will keep a record of questions that customers have called to ask in the past. Or a bank training a virtual assistant to answer questions about savings accounts will keep a record of questions customers have typed into chat windows on the bank's website. Both businesses can use these examples of real questions phrased by real people to train their ML models.

We saw in Chapter 3 that ML models give better answers when trained with data that is similar to what the project will need to do. You learned that if you want an ML model to recognize photos of different animals, you should train it with photos, and if you want it to recognize cartoons, you should train it with cartoons.

Text ML models work in a similar way. When we train them with questions phrased in the way that real people ask questions, they'll give better answers. The best way to do this for real-world ML projects is to find existing examples rather than making them up like we're doing for this project.

6. Click **Back to project** in the top-left corner of the screen.

7. Click **Learn & Test**, as shown in Figure 11-8.

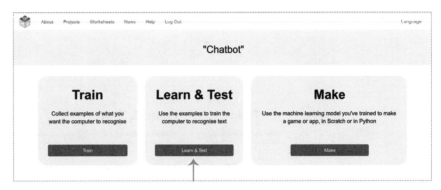

Figure 11-8: Learn & Test is the second phase of an ML project.

8. Click **Train new machine learning model**, as shown in Figure 11-9.

The computer will use the examples you've written to learn how to recognize questions that people ask about your topic. This process might take a minute or so. The computer is using this time to learn what the questions in each training bucket have in common, such as the words you used, the way you phrased the questions, how short or long the questions are, and much more.

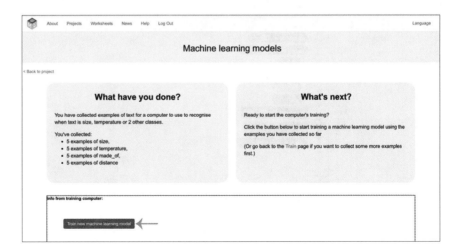

Figure 11-9: Train an ML model using the examples that you've written.

PREPARE YOUR PROJECT

Now that you have a character and an ML model, it's time to combine them to create your chatbot.

1. Click **Back to project** in the top-left corner of the screen.
2. Click **Make**, as shown in Figure 11-10.

Figure 11-10: Make is the third phase of an ML project.

3. Click **Scratch 3**, and then click **Open in Scratch 3**. Scratch will open with a new set of blocks for your Chatbot ML project.
4. Click **File ▶ Load from your computer**, as shown in Figure 11-11, to open the project you saved earlier with your chatbot scene.

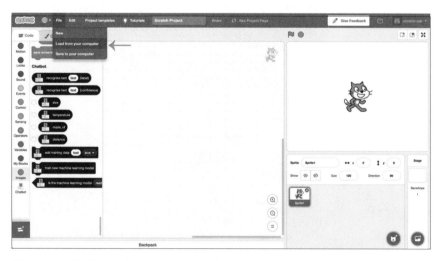

Figure 11-11: Open the project with the scene you created before.

5. Copy the script shown in Figure 11-12.

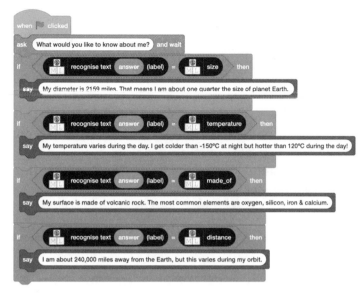

Figure 11-12: Sample script to create a simple chatbot

This script will ask you to type in a question and then use the ML model you've trained to recognize what you asked.

Your script should differ from mine, as mine has the questions about the moon that I trained my ML model with. Be sure to use your question types instead.

You'll also need to put the answers to the questions on your topic here. If you don't know them, now's the time to do some research to find the answers your chatbot should give!

6. Click **File ▶ Save to your computer** to save your project.

TEST YOUR PROJECT

Click the Green Flag and try asking your chatbot a question. Does it give you the right answer?

REVIEW AND IMPROVE YOUR PROJECT

You've created a simple chatbot that can recognize and answer the most common questions about a topic of your choice. Well done!

What could you do to improve your chatbot?

RESPONDING AND RECORDING WHEN USERS REPORT MISTAKES

AI systems cannot correctly understand everything, so you could improve your ML project by training it to handle mistakes. A good way to handle mistakes is to train your ML model to recognize when someone complains about the results it gives.

Go back to the Train phase and add a new training bucket called **mistake**. Fill it with examples of how someone might complain that the ML model got something wrong, as shown in Figure 11-13.

For example, you might add **That's not what I meant** to the mistake bucket.

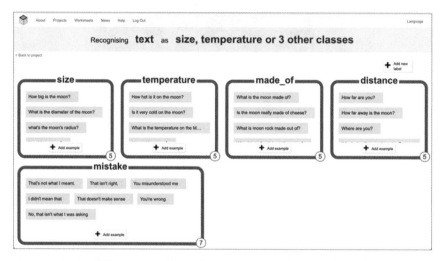

Figure 11-13: Collect examples of how a user might complain about a mistake the model makes.

Once you've added at least five examples, you'll need to return to the Learn & Test phase to train a new ML model.

NOTE   *You'll also need to close and reopen Scratch so it can use commands from the mistake bucket. Make sure you save your project before you close it so that you don't have to build your script again.*

When your chatbot recognizes that someone complains, the simplest response it can give is to apologize to them. Update your script as shown in Figure 11-14.

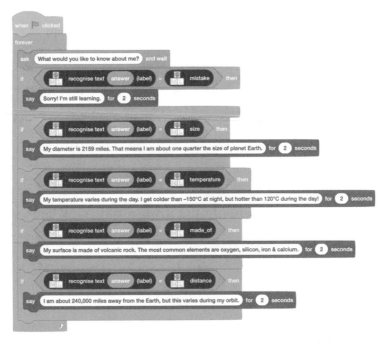

Figure 11-14: Update your script so that it apologizes if the user complains.

You can make your project even better by keeping a record of the mistakes. For example, I created a new list called mistakes (to do this, click **Variables** in the Toolbox, click **Make a List**, and enter the name **mistakes**) and updated the script as shown in Figure 11-15 so that if someone complains about the answer they get, their question is added to the list.

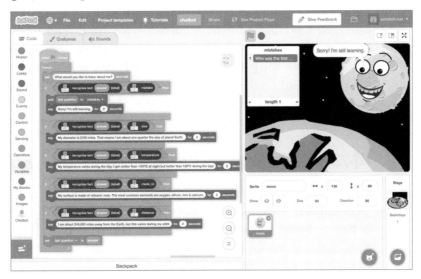

Figure 11-15: Keep a record of questions that the chatbot gets wrong.

When I asked, "Who was the first man on the moon?" my model told me how far the moon is from the Earth. Then, when I replied with, "No, that isn't what I asked for," my question about the first man on the moon was added to the mistakes list.

Tracking mistakes is a common technique used to improve real-world ML projects. The list of mistakes is used as a collection of examples to train the next version of the ML model.

What else could you do to improve your chatbot?

RECOGNIZING WHEN A USER ISN'T HAPPY

Your chatbot users might not always tell you when your ML system gets something wrong. So are there other ways that you can tell when it makes mistakes?

In Chapter 7, you learned about training an ML model to recognize tone and emotion in writing. You could combine that technique with this project to make your chatbot recognize when users are getting angry or annoyed.

Train two ML models: one to recognize the meaning of questions (as you've just done) and the other to recognize emotion (such as "annoyed" and "not annoyed," similar to your project in Chapter 7). If the second ML model has a high degree of confidence that the user sounds annoyed, your chatbot should apologize instead of trying to answer the question again.

Detecting the user's tone, and apologizing when necessary, is a common technique used for chatbots that communicate with members of the public, such as for customer service. People can get annoyed if some technology consistently misunderstands them. If systems can recognize when things are going badly and apologize, the customer may be happier. In such cases, these systems will also commonly call for a human customer service representative or manager to join the conversation and help.

Is there anything else you could do to improve your project?

ANSWERING ONLY WHEN THE ML MODEL IS CONFIDENT

Recognizing when the user is annoyed is a good thing. But it's often better to avoid annoying the user in the first place! You can use the confidence score to prevent your chatbot from giving wrong answers.

You learned in Chapter 7 that the confidence score is a percentage returned by an ML model that shows how confident the model is that it has correctly recognized whatever it's been trained on.

In this project, if the confidence score is low, it means the ML model isn't sure that it understood the question. You could modify your chatbot code as shown in Figure 11-16 so that if the model doesn't understand the question, the chatbot apologizes rather than simply guessing the answer, and the question gets added to the list of examples to train the model with in the future.

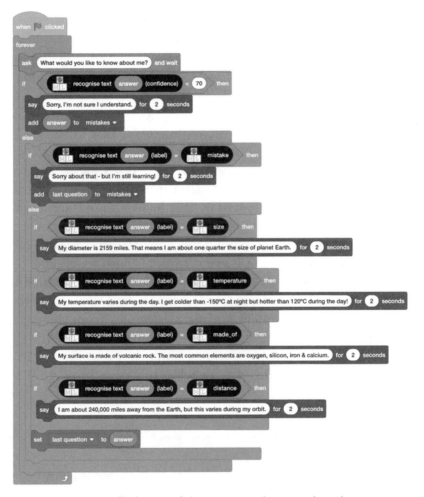

Figure 11-16: Handle low confidence scores by recording the questions to use in future training.

ML AND ETHICS

These suggestions for improving your project are based on common real-world approaches to ML projects. As you've seen, collecting training data takes a lot of time and effort. To save time, some companies using ML collect just enough training examples to make an ML model basically work, and then allow their customers to start using it (sometimes describing it as a *beta* to explain why it still gets some things wrong). Then they collect poor experiences their customers have with their ML model so that they can improve their training data. This might mean collecting examples of customer questions that the ML model had a low confidence score in, or where the customer reported that the answer was unhelpful. The company then reviews these customer questions and sorts them into the right training buckets.

Companies say they do this because it means their ML model will do a better job of answering questions in the future. The more representative they make the training examples they use, the better answers their system can give. But sometimes this surprises people who don't realize that questions they ask their smart devices can be recorded by the device's manufacturer. Try searching the web for news stories about the maker of your favorite smart device listening to what people ask the device. How many articles can you find? What do you think of these reactions?

What do you think this means for the responsibilities of the people who create ML systems? Do you think it's ethical for ML developers to collect training examples from their customers or users? Do you think they should tell users that this is happening? And how would you explain it to users who might not realize what training examples are, or why they're so important for training ML systems?

WHAT YOU LEARNED

In this chapter, you learned that ML models can be trained to understand and respond to questions people ask. You learned the differences between question answering (QA) systems and their simpler counterpart, chatbots. You then designed a custom chatbot and trained an ML model to recognize the most common questions about a topic of your choosing. You saw a few different ways you could extend your chatbot to improve its performance and accuracy, such as by tracking mistakes, responding appropriately to customers' feedback and tone, and using the confidence score to decide when a question should be directed to a person (for example, in a customer service setting). Finally, you learned about some of the ethical questions to consider when training ML models with feedback from real people.

In the next chapter, we'll switch gears and train an ML model for the first time to recognize numbers in a simplified version of the video game *Pac-Man*.

12

AVOIDING THE MONSTER

AI and ML have exciting potential for the future of computer games, such as computer game characters that learn to understand your words and actions. There are already games where characters behave like the chatbots you learned about in the last chapter. However, the opportunity for truly intelligent games that adapt as they are played is enormous.

In this chapter, we'll look at the reverse situation: not how AI can contribute to game development, but how games have been used in AI development.

Games provide a simulation environment with a well-defined goal, a way to collect training examples, and a way to measure effectiveness, which makes them a great platform for the research and development of computer systems that can learn.

Pac-Man (and *Ms. Pac-Man*) is an example of a classic computer game that has regularly been used in AI research. The *Ms. Pac-Man AI competition*, where academics submit ML systems that compete to see which is best at playing the game, has been held multiple times since 2007 and is still used as a task for AI students and researchers today.

In this chapter, you'll try training an ML system to play a simplified version of *Pac-Man*, where the objective is to navigate a character through a maze while avoiding a monster (see Figure 12-1).

Let's get started!

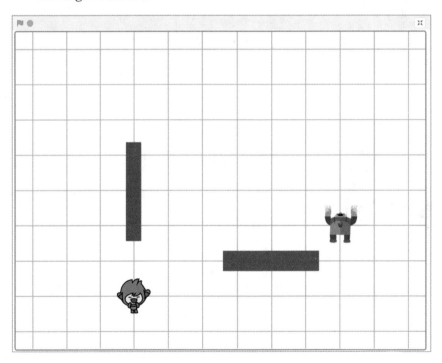

Figure 12-1: A simple video game we can train an ML system to play

BUILD YOUR PROJECT

Before we start, try the game for yourself so you understand what we'll be training the computer to do. First, go to *https://machinelearningforkids.co.uk/scratch3/* and click **Project templates** in the top menu bar, as shown in Figure 12-2.

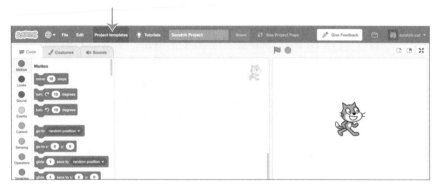

*Figure 12-2: Access the game from the **Project templates** menu.*

Click the **Avoid the monster** game as shown in Figure 12-3.

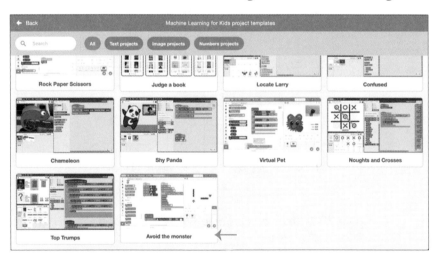

*Figure 12-3: Click **Avoid the monster** in the list of project templates.*

In this game, you play as the character *nano*, which starts off in the bottom-left corner of the Stage. Your objective is to avoid the monster, which starts off in the top-right corner of the Stage, for as long as you can.

You control nano using the arrow keys to change direction. Nano can only follow the grid, so you can only move up, down, left, and right. You can't move diagonally.

When you're not pressing an arrow key, nano will just continue in whatever direction you last pressed.

Nano can't move faster than the monster. The game's code uses a timer so that both nano and the monster can make only one move per second.

There are two walls in the way. Neither nano nor the monster is allowed to go through the walls.

Give the game a try. Click the full-screen icon in the controls at the top right and then click the Green Flag.

How long can you avoid the monster?

DESCRIBE THE STATE OF THE GAME

The game board can be represented as a graph, as shown in Figure 12-4.

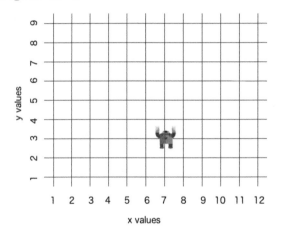

Figure 12-4: Think of the game board as a graph with x- and y-axes.

Using this graph, you can describe the locations of nano and the monster as a pair of coordinates. For example, in Figure 12-4 the monster is at $x = 7$ and $y = 3$.

We'll use this representation of the game to describe it to the computer.

We want to give the computer four numbers so that it can decide to move nano up, down, left, or right to avoid the monster.

For example, if we input the coordinates shown in Figure 12-5, the computer could decide to move nano up.

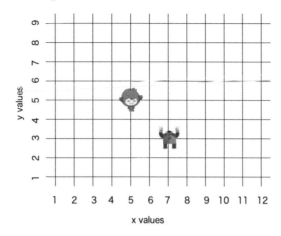

Figure 12-5: Nano is at x = 5, y = 5, and the monster is at x = 7, y = 3.

Your objective for this project is to train an ML model to decide on the best direction to avoid the monster.

TRAIN YOUR MODEL

To train the computer to play the game, you need to collect examples of the game being played. The best way to do this is to play the game yourself and use your playing to train the computer.

The first step is to prepare the training buckets where you'll store examples of the moves you make.

1. Go to *https://machinelearningforkids.co.uk/*. Create a new ML project, name it **Avoid the monster**, and set it to learn to recognize numbers.

NOTE   *If you're not sure how to create an ML project, read the section "Creating a New ML Project" on page 9 in Chapter 2.*

2. Click **Add a value**, type **nano x** for the value name, and set **Type of value** to **number**. Click **Add another value** and then add three more values named **nano y**, **monster x**, and **monster y**, as shown in Figure 12-6. Once you've added all four values, click **Create**.

These values will store the coordinates of the two characters on the graph.

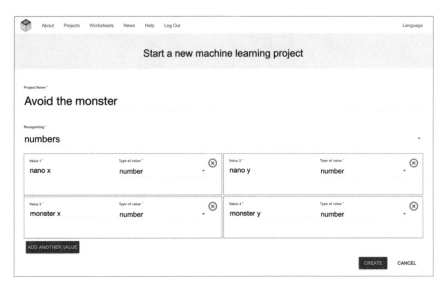

Figure 12-6: Prepare the values for the Avoid the monster project.

3. Click **Train**, as shown in Figure 12-7.

Figure 12-7: Click **Train** to prepare your training buckets.

4. Click **Add new label**, as shown in Figure 12-8, and create four training buckets for the four directions nano can move. Call them **go left**, **go right**, **go up**, and **go down**. (The underscores will be added automatically.)

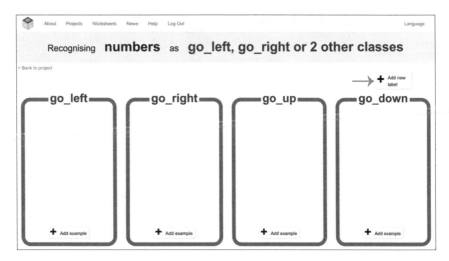

Figure 12-8: Prepare four training buckets for the four directions nano can move.

For example, imagine nano is at coordinates $x = 2$, $y = 3$ and the monster is at the coordinates $x = 6$, $y = 7$ while you're playing the game. If you pressed the right arrow to move nano to the right, that set of numbers would be added to the go_right training bucket, as shown in Figure 12-9.

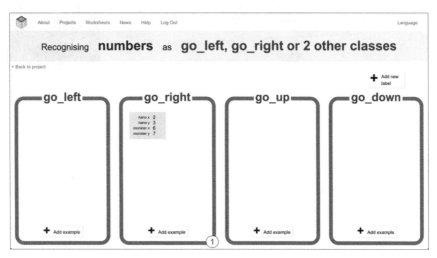

Figure 12-9: Moves that you make while playing the game will be added to the training buckets.

The next step is to collect lots and lots of examples that we can use to train an ML model. We'll collect training examples by playing the game.

5. Click **Back to project** and then click **Make**, as shown in Figure 12-10.

*Figure 12-10: Click **Make** to use your project in Scratch.*

6. Click **Scratch 3**, as shown in Figure 12-11.

*Figure 12-11: Click **Scratch 3** to go back to Scratch.*

7. Click **straight into Scratch**, as shown in Figure 12-12.

NOTE   *The page will warn you that you don't have an ML model yet, but that's fine—you'll be using Scratch to collect training data.*

8. Click **Project templates** in the top menu bar.
9. Click **Avoid the monster** to open the template again, this time with blocks from your ML project.

*Figure 12-12: Click **straight into Scratch** even though you don't have an ML model yet.*

10. Click the **Stage** backdrop at the bottom right of the screen. In the Code Area, find the first **When Green Flag clicked** script, as shown in Figure 12-13.

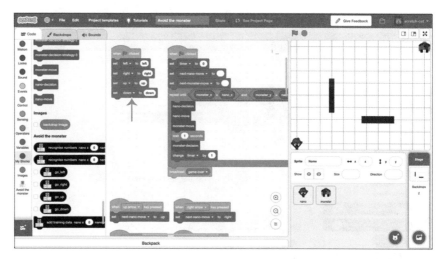

Figure 12-13: Find the first, shorter green flag script in the Code Area.

11. In the Toolbox, click **Avoid the monster** and drag the blocks with the names of your training buckets into the script as shown in Figure 12-14. Make sure the directions match; for example, drag **go_left** into the **set left to** block.

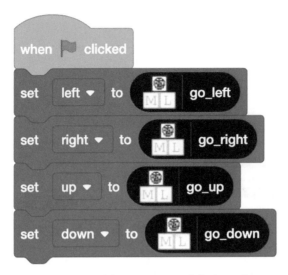

Figure 12-14: Add your project labels to the script.

12. Scroll down in the Code Area to find the **define nano-decision** script, as shown in Figure 12-15.

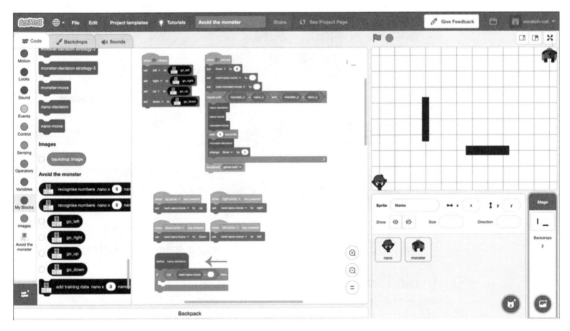

Figure 12-15: Find the **define nano-decision** script.

13. From the **Avoid the monster** group in the Toolbox, drag a new **add training data** block to the script, as shown in Figure 12-16. This block will add every move that you make while playing the game to your training examples.

Click **Variables** in the Toolbox and drag the blocks shown in Figure 12-16 into the **add training data** block. For each move, the coordinates for your character and the monster will be added, together with the decision you made, to your training examples.

Figure 12-16: Update the **define nano-decision** script.

14. Now you need to save your project so that you can return to it later. First, in the **Scratch Project** text box in the top menu bar, type **Avoid the monster TRAINING** as shown in Figure 12-17. This tells you that this version of the project is where you play the game to train your ML model.

Then click **File ▶ Save to your computer**.

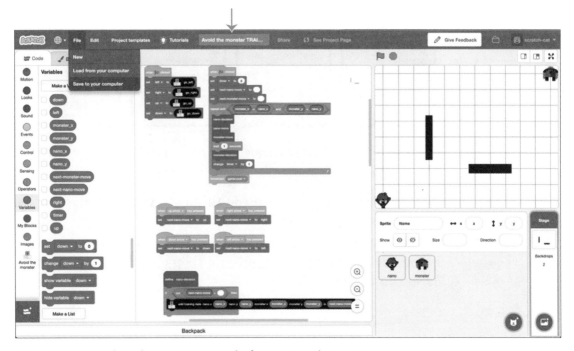

Figure 12-17: Update the project name before saving this version.

15. Play the game!

In the controls at the top right of the screen, click the full-screen icon and then click the Green Flag to start the game. Use the arrow keys to control the nano character like you did before.

Do your best to avoid the monster for as long as possible. The better you play, the better the ML model can learn.

When you think you've played for long enough, click the red Stop Sign.

You can see the moves that you've made if you go back to the Train phase, as shown in Figure 12-18. You may need to refresh the page to see the latest examples.

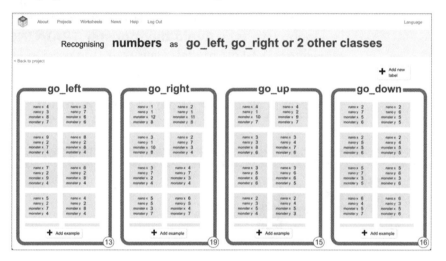

Figure 12-18: Moves that you made while playing should be displayed in your training buckets.

16. Play a few more games until you think you've collected examples of all the situations nano could get into.

17. It's time to train an ML model using the examples you've collected. Click **Back to project** and then click **Learn & Test**, as shown in Figure 12-19.

Figure 12-19: Click **Learn & Test** to train a model using the moves you've collected.

18. Click **Train new machine learning model**, as shown in Figure 12-20.

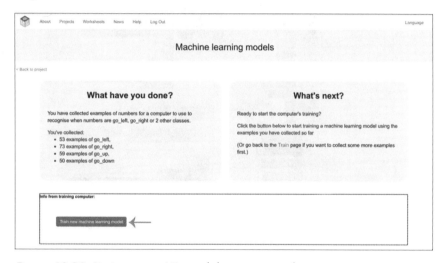

Figure 12-20: Train a new ML model using your playing moves.

TEST YOUR GAME

You've trained an ML model to play the game! The best way to test your model is to let the ML model take control of the nano character and see how long it can avoid the monster for.

We'll need to modify our Scratch project so that it can be controlled by the ML model, not the arrow keys.

1. Find the **when arrow key pressed** scripts in the Code Area. There are four of them, as shown in Figure 12-21: **when left arrow key pressed**, **when right arrow key pressed**, **when up arrow key pressed**, and **when down arrow key pressed**.

   Delete the scripts either by clicking each block and pressing the DELETE key or by right-clicking each block and choosing **Delete Block**. Be sure to delete every block in all four scripts so that you can't take control of the character with any arrow key.

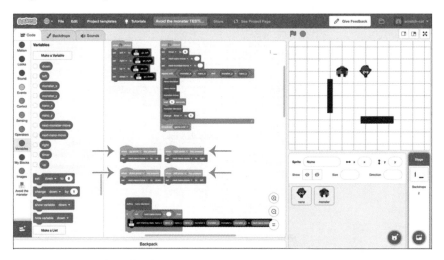

*Figure 12-21: Delete the four **when arrow key pressed** scripts so you can no longer control nano.*

2. Find the **define nano-decision** block that you updated before. Using blocks from the **Variables** and **Avoid the monster** groups in the Toolbox, update the script again so that it looks like Figure 12-22.

   Instead of learning from your arrow keys, now you want the computer to make decisions using your ML model.

*Figure 12-22: Update the **define nano-decision** script so that your ML model is controlling the game.*

3. Find the longer **when Green Flag clicked** script and remove the **wait 1 second** block.

This will make the game run a little quicker so that you don't have to wait for each move. The updated script will look like Figure 12-23. (The arrow shows where the block was before I removed it.)

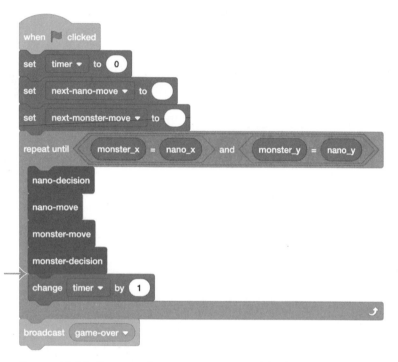

*Figure 12-23: Remove the **wait 1 second** block.*

4. Now you need to save your project again so that you can return to it later. This time, enter the name **Avoid the monster TESTING** in the text box so you'll know that this version of the project is where you let the ML model play. Then, click **File ▶ Save to your computer**.

5. Click the full-screen icon and then click the Green Flag.

Watch your ML model try to keep nano safe from the monster (Figure 12-24)!

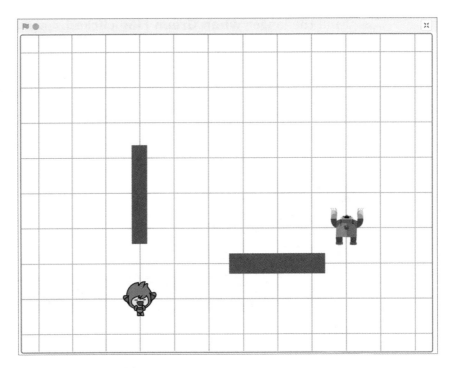

Figure 12-24: Your ML project in action

REVIEW AND IMPROVE YOUR PROJECT

How did your ML model do?

The longer it managed to avoid the monster, the better it did. If you've done really well, it'll be able to avoid the monster forever. Because the monster moves at the same speed as nano, as long as your ML model doesn't make any mistakes, it's possible for nano to always stay ahead of the monster.

What difference does the amount of training make?

Try opening your *training* version of the Scratch project and add more training examples by playing the game for a little longer. Then, go back to the Learn & Test phase and train a new ML model using your extra training examples. Finally, open your *testing* version of the Scratch project and watch the new ML model play the game.

Did the extra training help?

Try doing this a few times to see how the amount of training affects how well your ML model plays.

The type of ML model you've trained in this project is called a *decision tree classifier*, because the way the model makes decisions about its next moves can be drawn as a sort of tree, as shown in Figure 12-25. To see a diagram of your ML model, in the Learn & Test phase, click **Describe your model!** next to the Test button.

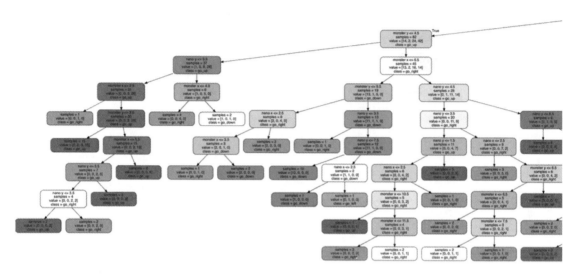

Figure 12-25: A decision tree

The decision tree diagram can help you understand how your ML model is making *predictions* about the outcome of each move.

Each box on the tree describes a test; for example, monster x < 3 means "is the x-coordinate of the monster less than 3?" If the test is true, the tree follows the left-hand arrow. If the test is not true, the tree follows the right-hand arrow.

The ML model starts at the top of the tree and follows the arrows identified by the tests until it reaches the bottom of the tree.

To see an example of the decision process, enter some coordinates for nano and the monster into the boxes to the right of your decision tree, and click **Test**. The diagram will highlight the way your ML model made a prediction for those coordinates. When there are no more arrows to follow and it reaches the bottom of the tree, you'll find the final prediction, as shown in Figure 12-26.

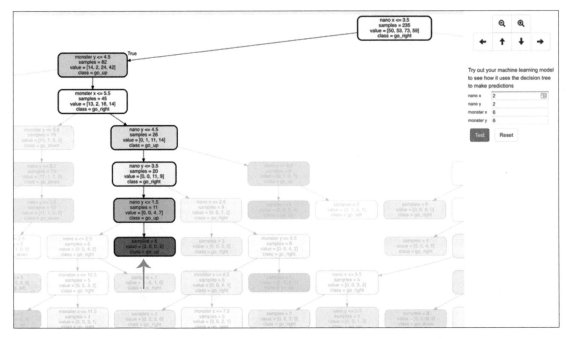

Figure 12-26: Highlighting the coordinates used to make a prediction about the outcome of a move

Test your model with a few different sets of coordinates to understand how it has learned to make predictions.

WHAT YOU LEARNED

In this chapter, you learned that ML models can be trained to recognize patterns in sets of numbers. You used a decision tree classifier to train a model to play a simplified version of the game *Pac-Man*, using sets of x- and y-coordinates to make decisions about its next moves based on their predicted outcome.

A decision tree is not the only way to train an ML model to make predictions based on numbers, but it's a popular choice because it's very quick to train and one of the easiest techniques to understand. In previous chapters, you've been using neural networks, which can be more powerful but are more complicated and harder to understand.

You've seen that, as with other ML models you've trained before, the model's performance improves as you collect more training examples. In the next chapter, you'll learn more about the difference the amount of training data makes on ML projects.

13
TIC TAC TOE

n the last chapter, you saw how computer games like *Pac-Man* have been used in ML development. Tic Tac Toe (also known as Noughts and Crosses, or Xs and Os) has been used to help people learn about ML for even longer.

For example, Donald Michie, a British AI researcher, designed *MENACE*, the *Machine Educable Noughts and Crosses Engine*, in 1960 (see Figure 13-1). It was one of the first programs that was able to learn how to play Tic Tac Toe perfectly. MENACE was demonstrated using matchboxes and colored glass beads, and it is a good reminder that many of the principles behind ML have been developed over many decades.

Figure 13-1: A re-creation of Donald Michie's Machine Educable Noughts and Crosses Engine, or MENACE (source: Matthew Scroggs, https://commons .wikimedia.org/wiki/File:Mscroggs-MENACE-cropped.jpg)

Tic Tac Toe is not the only game that has been used to drive AI development, however. Chess is another good example. In Chapter 1, I mentioned Deep Blue, the IBM computer that beat the chess grandmaster Garry Kasparov. This followed decades of work to build computers that could play chess. As early as the 1950s, mathematician Alan Turing wrote a paper called "Digital Computers Applied to Games" in which he asked, "Could one make a machine to play chess, and to improve its play, game by game, profiting from its experience?"

In more recent years, the AI community has turned its attention to more complex games, like the board game *Go*. Because of the huge number of potential moves and strategies in *Go*, it's impossible to rely on the "brute-force" approach of computers like Deep Blue (which examine all possible future moves and positions). Google DeepMind's computer AlphaGo achieved a milestone in AI research in 2016, when it defeated *Go* world champion Lee Sedol.

The tools for creating neural networks are getting easier to use, and our computers are becoming faster and more powerful, moving beyond the realms of AI students and researchers. If you do a web search for "Super Mario neural network," you'll find dozens of examples and tutorials of training ML models to play games like *Super Mario World.*

In this chapter, though, we'll stick to the basics. We'll be building a simplified version of Donald Michie's MENACE design in Scratch and training an ML model to play Tic Tac Toe (see Figure 13-2).

Figure 13-2: Tic Tac Toe is a great game for ML research.

Let's get started!

BUILD YOUR PROJECT

You probably know how to play Tic Tac Toe already, but let's quickly try it out in Scratch so we can plan how to introduce ML into it.

Go to *https://machinelearningforkids.co.uk/scratch3/* and click **Project templates** in the top menu bar, as shown in Figure 13-3.

In the list of templates, click **Noughts and Crosses**. The template loads a simple Tic Tac Toe game in Scratch. Click the Green Flag to give it a try.

You're placing crosses (X) and the computer is placing noughts (O). The computer strategy isn't very clever, but you'll be making it more intelligent in this chapter.

Figure 13-3: Access the project templates from the top menu.

Try to figure out the rules that the computer is following. The logic for where the computer moves next is all in the Code Area, so you can review the scripts there to see if you're right.

There are many ways to represent the game board, but to start with we'll use a very simple approach: numbering each of the cells on the board from 1 to 9, as shown in Figure 13-4.

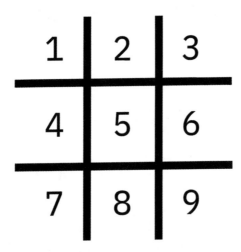

Figure 13-4: One approach to representing the game board is to number the cells.

The cells are also represented with numbers in the Scratch project template, as you can see in Figure 13-5.

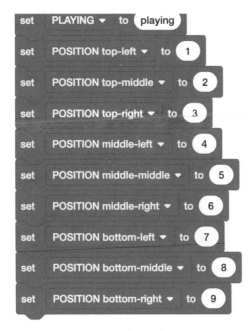

Figure 13-5: Game board representation
defined in the Scratch project template

We also need to describe the positions of the noughts and crosses on the board. We'll want to be able to learn from whoever wins (whether it's noughts or crosses who wins a game), so to keep things clear, we'll use *player* to describe the winning moves and *opponent* to describe the losing moves.

For example, imagine that the board looked like Figure 13-6 early in a game that cross (X) ended up winning.

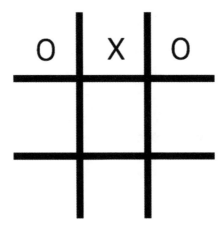

Figure 13-6: An example game board state

We can describe this board as follows:

Top left	Opponent
Top middle	Player
Top right	Opponent
Middle left	Empty
Middle middle	Empty
Middle right	Empty
Bottom left	Empty
Bottom middle	Empty
Bottom right	Empty

We want to train an ML model so that, given the state of a board like this, it can choose where to make the next move. To be able to do that, we'll need training examples of decisions that led to a win. Each example will need to include:

▶ What the board looked like before a move
▶ What move was made

Training examples will be recorded only for moves made by the player that won that game. If you (cross) win the game, you want to train the model with the cross (X) moves. If the computer (nought) wins the game, you want to train it with the nought (O) moves.

PREPARE YOUR GAME

As with the *Pac-Man*–style game in the last chapter, the best way to collect training examples isn't by typing them, but by playing the game yourself.

The first step is to prepare the training buckets where you'll store examples of the moves you make. You will need nine training buckets: one for each possible choice available at any point in the game.

1. Go to *https://machinelearningforkids.co.uk/*. Create a new ML project, name it **Tic Tac Toe**, and set it to learn to recognize numbers.

NOTE *If you're not sure how to create an ML project, read the section "Creating a New ML Project" on page 9 in Chapter 2.*

2. Click **Add a value**, type **TopLeft** for the value name, and set **Type of value** to **multiple-choice**. Under **Choices**, add three choices: **EMPTY**, **PLAYER**, and **OPPONENT**. Then click **Add another value** and add eight more multiple-choice values with the same three choices:

> **TopMiddle**
>
> **TopRight**
>
> **MiddleLeft**
>
> **MiddleMiddle**
>
> **MiddleRight**
>
> **BottomLeft**
>
> **BottomMiddle**
>
> **BottomRight**

Make sure that you spell the choices *exactly* the same for all nine values so that the computer will know that the choices available are the same for every space on the game board. If you make a typing mistake, click the red X beside the choice to delete it, and then add it again.

When you've finished, your screen should look like Figure 13-7.

Figure 13-7: Preparing the project

3.   Click **Create**.

4.   Click **Train**, as shown in Figure 13-8.

*Figure 13-8: Click **Train** to prepare the training buckets.*

5.   Click **Add new label**, as shown in Figure 13-9, and create nine training buckets to represent the nine cells on the game board. Call them **top left**, **top middle**, **top right**, **middle left**, **middle middle**, **middle right**, **bottom left**, **bottom middle**, and **bottom right**. (The underscores will be added automatically.)

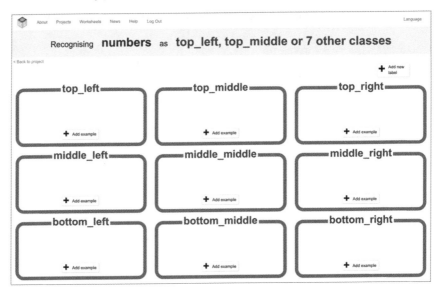

Figure 13-9: Training buckets for Tic Tac Toe

These buckets are where your training examples will be stored. For example, look back at the state of the game board shown in Figure 13-6. If the player's next move (X) went in the middle_middle cell, the board's state would be recorded in the training data as shown in Figure 13-10.

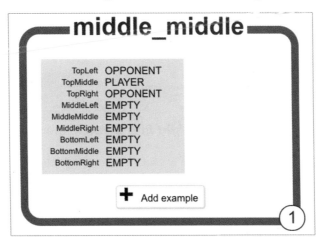

Figure 13-10: A training example for Tic Tac Toe

The next step is to collect lots and lots of examples to train an ML model.

6. Click **Back to project** in the top-left corner of the screen.

7. Click **Make**.

8. Click **Scratch 3** and then click **straight into Scratch**, as shown in Figure 13-11.

NOTE *The page will warn you that you don't have an ML model yet, but that's okay—you'll be using Scratch to collect your training data.*

*Figure 13-11: Click **straight into Scratch**, even though we don't have an ML model yet.*

9. Open the **Noughts and Crosses** project template again.

    The code is the same as when you opened this template before, but now you have extra blocks for your project in the Toolbox.

10. Click the **Stage** backdrop at the bottom right of the screen. In the Code Area, find the **setup model labels** script shown in Figure 13-12. This script sets up constants that are used throughout the project.

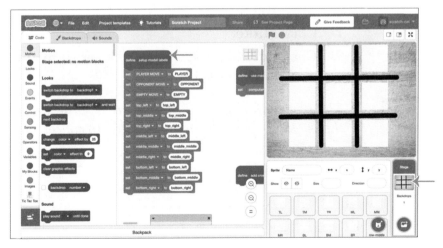

*Figure 13-12: Find the **setup model labels** script.*

11. In the Toolbox, click **Tic Tac Toe** and drag the blocks with the names of your training buckets into the **setup model labels** script as shown in Figure 13-13. Make sure the positions match; for example, drag **top_left** into the **set top_left to** block.

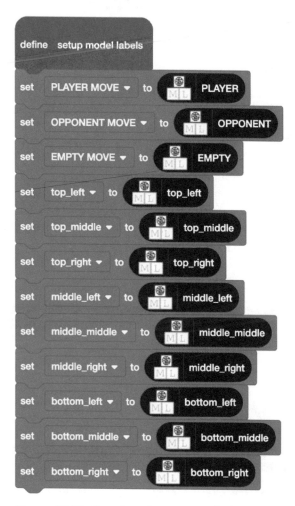

Figure 13-13: Populate the script with the training bucket names from your project.

12. Scroll in the Code Area to find the **define add cross moves to training data** and **define add nought moves to training data** script blocks, as shown in Figure 13-14.

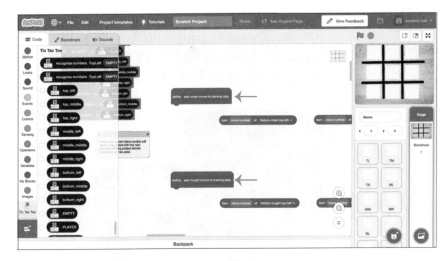

*Figure 13-14: Find the custom **define** blocks.*

13. From the **Tic Tac Toe** group in the Toolbox, drag an **add training data** block into both of the **define** scripts, as shown in Figure 13-15.

*Figure 13-15: Add training data to both of the **define** scripts.*

14. Update the **add training data** blocks as shown in Figure 13-16. The orange blocks you need are ready for you in the project template, immediately below where they need to go. *Starting from the left*, drag each block into the space above it.

Figure 13-16: Populate the training data blocks.

Double-check the scripts. The moves from the history cross lists should appear in the add cross moves to training data script, as shown in Figure 13-17.

Figure 13-17: Check that you've matched the cross blocks with the cross script.

Likewise, the moves from the history nought lists should be used in the add nought moves to training data script.

The names for the spaces on the game board should also match. For example, the top-middle move goes into the TopMiddle space, as shown in Figure 13-18.

Figure 13-18: Check that you've matched the names for the game board spaces.

Make sure you fill all of the spaces in the blocks. You'll need to scroll to the right to do this, as you can see in Figure 13-19.

Figure 13-19: Make sure you fill in all of the spaces.

15. Now find the **when I receive game over** script, as shown in Figure 13-20. This script runs at the end of each game and is responsible for calling the add moves to training data scripts you've just set up.

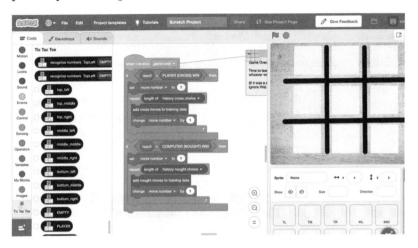

*Figure 13-20: Find the **when I receive game over** script.*

Add a new **train new machine learning model** block to the end of the **when I receive game over** script, as shown in Figure 13-21.

Figure 13-21: Train a new ML model after every game.

Now, at the end of every game, the winner's moves will be added to the training buckets, and you'll use that updated set of training examples to train a new ML model. This means that your ML model should get a little smarter, and a little better, after every game you play.

TRAIN YOUR MODEL

It's time to play!

1. Click the full-screen icon and then the Green Flag in the controls at the top right of the screen. Play *one* game of Tic Tac Toe, as shown in Figure 13-22.

Figure 13-22: Play a game of Tic Tac Toe.

2. After the game, click **Back to project** and then **Train**. You should see all of the moves made by the winning player, as shown in Figure 13-23.

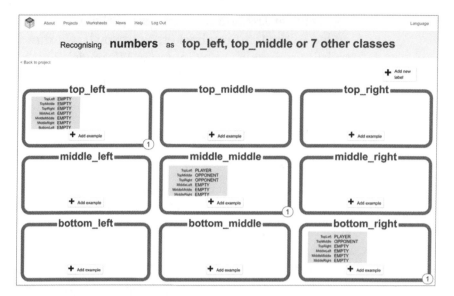

Figure 13-23: Compare the training data with the game in Figure 13-22.

3. Now that you have an ML model, it's time to update the Scratch game so that the computer can use the model to decide where to make its moves. Scroll through the Code Area to find the **define use machine learning model** script, as shown in Figure 13-24.

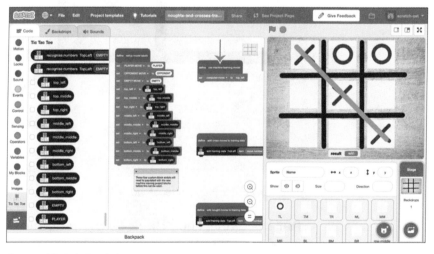

Figure 13-24: Find the **define use machine learning model** script.

Update the script as shown in Figure 13-25 so that it uses your ML model to recognize the best move for the computer to make.

Figure 13-25: Add the **recognise numbers (label)** block to the script.

Make sure that you use the recognise numbers (label) block, not the recognise numbers (confidence) block. You want to use what the ML model thinks is the best choice, not how confident the model is about that.

4. Drag the orange blocks into the **recognise numbers (label)** block, as shown in Figure 13-26. As before, these are ready for you in the template immediately underneath where they should go. This code block will give the game board's current state to the ML model so that the model can use that information to recognize the best next move.

   Make sure that you add all nine blocks, for all nine spaces on the game board, and work from left to right. Also be sure that the block names match up. For example, current state top-middle goes into the TopMiddle space.

Figure 13-26: Make sure that you match the block names correctly.

TEST YOUR GAME

It's time to test your project!

Because you've coded your project to learn as you play, you should see the computer get better at the game over time. But how can you verify if that actually happens?

One way is to play a lot of games, keep a count of the number of times the computer wins, and plot whether the number increases with the amount of training you gave the ML model.

I played 300 games of Tic Tac Toe and counted the number of matches that I won, lost, and tied. I plotted the results in the bar chart shown in Figure 13-27. Each column represents 10 games of Tic Tac Toe. Green represents games that I won. Orange represents games that ended in a tie. Red represents games won by the ML system.

The bar on the far left represents the first 10 games that I played. I won all 10 of them.

The next bar represents the next 10 games that I played. I won all 10 of those, too.

The bar on the far right represents the last 10 games that I played. I won 2 games, tied 4 games, and lost 4 games.

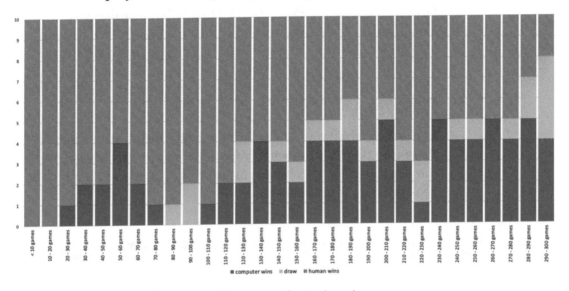

Figure 13-27: The results from Tic Tac Toe games that I played

My first 10 games were very easy to win. The computer made foolish moves, and I didn't have to try hard to win. By my last 10 games, however, it was harder to win. I had to concentrate and not make a single mistake to win a game. Although my feelings can't be shown on the graph, it *felt* to me like the computer was getting better as I played.

Every ML project will go a little differently, so try training your own model and measuring how your project learns and improves. Hopefully you'll see that the more training examples you collect, the better your ML model performs. But you'll almost certainly see some variation in that, as I did.

REVIEW AND IMPROVE YOUR PROJECT

You created an ML system that learns to play Tic Tac Toe by competing against you. The biggest challenge with training the system yourself is the time it takes to play hundreds of training games. Are there more efficient ways to get more training examples?

One common way is to get more people to help. Imagine if, instead of playing the 300 games myself, I had saved my Scratch project and gave the project file to 30 friends and asked them to play 10 games each. Dividing the work would have made training much easier, as playing only 10 games would be very quick for each person.

Now imagine if I could get 300 people to help, or 3,000!

Hopefully you can see the benefits of spreading the work of training an ML model across a large number of people. This is sometimes described as *crowdsourcing*. There are some challenges with that, too, like being able to find a large group of people, coordinating them, explaining what you want to all of them, making sure they all do what you want and don't train your ML model to do things you don't want, and so on. But even so, using many people for training is still the best option for a lot of complicated projects.

WHAT YOU LEARNED

In this chapter, you learned that Tic Tac Toe, or Noughts and Crosses, has been used to help people understand ML for decades. You trained an ML model to recognize numbers and built a Tic Tac Toe board with numbered cells representing each move. This project was based on the 1960 work of British AI researcher Donald Michie, who used matchboxes and glass beads in his MENACE project. Each matchbox represented a possible state of the game board, similar to the examples that you collected in your training data. The number of beads in the matchboxes was like the number of times an example shows up in one of the training buckets.

You also saw the importance of having lots of training examples to improve your ML model's performance over time. Because the training set is updated with the winner's moves after each game, the model gradually gets better and more difficult to beat. You learned that it can be useful to crowdsource, or share the work of training the model across a large group of people, to save yourself some time and effort.

In the next chapter, you'll start to learn about how ML projects can go wrong.

14

CONFUSING THE
COMPUTER

ntil now, we've been focused on the
great things that we can do using ML,
and on the ways that it is being used
well in real-world applications. But, as you've seen
throughout this book, ML systems are not perfect
or all-knowing. Their behavior is determined by the
training that we give them. The way that we train

our ML systems will affect the responses that they give, and not always in a positive way. In this chapter, we'll look at one of the most common challenges in creating AI systems: *bias*.

The project in this chapter is based on an old story, sometimes described as the *Russian Tank problem*, that is often told to AI students. It's probably not true, but it illustrates the impact of bias in ML training sets.

Here's one example of how the story is told:

> Once upon a time, the US Army decided to use ML to recognize tanks hiding behind trees in the woods. Researchers trained an ML model using photos of woods without tanks, and photos of the same woods with tanks hiding behind trees.
>
> The model seemed to do well with the researchers' pictures, but when the US Army tested their system, it didn't do any better than random guesses.
>
> It turned out that in the researchers' training data, the photos of camouflaged tanks had been taken on a cloudy day, while photos of the plain forest had been taken on a sunny day. The ML model had learned to recognize cloudy days from sunny days, instead of recognizing camouflaged tanks.

Here's another version:

> Once upon a time, the US Army tried training a computer to recognize the difference between Russian and American tanks. Researchers trained an ML model using photos they took of American tanks and spy photos they collected of Russian tanks.
>
> The model seemed to do well with the researchers' pictures, but when the US Army tested their system, the ML model didn't do any better than random guesses.
>
> It turned out that the researchers' photos of American tanks were large, high resolution, and high quality. But the long-distance spy photos they were able to get of Russian tanks were all blurry, low resolution, and grainy.
>
> The ML model had learned to recognize the difference between grainy photos and high-quality photos, instead of between Russian and American tanks.

As another example, when researchers at Stanford University were developing an ML system to recognize skin cancers from photos, they accidentally created an ML model that recognized rulers, because medical photographs of skin cancers normally include a ruler to show the size of the lesion or tumor.

The point is that, due to unintentional bias, ML systems can learn to spot patterns that their creators might not have been aware of or that weren't intended to be treated as patterns.

In this chapter, you'll train an image classifier to recognize pictures of objects, but you'll introduce bias to make it get things wrong. We'll see firsthand what sorts of problems can cause an ML model to make mistakes, and then we'll talk about how we can avoid these problems and fix the model.

BUILD YOUR PROJECT

Choose two objects that you want to train the computer to recognize photographs of. Pick things that are obviously different. Don't choose anything too personal, as you'll need to upload the photos to the internet to do the project.

For my screenshots, I chose a lemon and a grapefruit that I found in my kitchen. You can choose anything you like, though.

Put the first object down somewhere and take 10 similar-looking photographs of it. You don't need the photos to be high resolution. Small photos (under 800 pixels in width) will work best.

I put my grapefruit down on a wooden floor in a dark room, and took the photos shown in Figure 14-1.

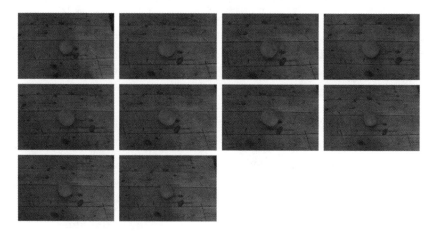

Figure 14-1: Photos of my first object, a grapefruit

Put the second object down somewhere different and take 10 photographs of it.

I put my lemon down on a cream-colored carpet in a bright, light room and took the photos shown in Figure 14-2.

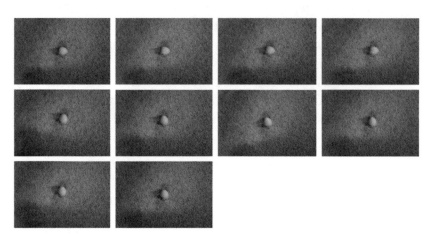

Figure 14-2: Photos of my second object, a lemon

Don't make the object too large in the photos. Try to keep the object in the same position in each photo, as shown in Figures 14-1 and 14-2.

The aim is to make all 10 photographs very similar *within each set*, but to make everything—the object, the background, the lighting—different *between the two sets*. For example, if your photos of the first object are on a dark background, take your photos of the second object on a light background. But all the photos of the first object should be on the dark background, and all of the photos of the second object should be on the light background.

Here are some other ideas for how you could make your two sets of photographs different.

If your photos of the first object are all...	Take all the photos of the second object...
on a *dark* background	on a *light* background
on *tiles*	on *grass*
brightly lit	*somewhere dark*
clear, crisp, and *focused*	*fuzzy* and *blurry*
outdoors with a garden in the background	*indoors* with the same room in the background

Have another look at my photos. The photos in Figure 14-1 have in common dark lighting, the dark brown surface, and the wooden pattern background. The photos in Figure 14-2 have in common bright lighting, the cream surface, and the speckled carpet background.

You don't have to copy my photos exactly. Be creative!

Once you've taken your 20 photos, you need to put them online somewhere to make them available for training. Choose any photo hosting web service that will let you upload photos to the internet for no charge. (If you already have an account with a photo sharing service, you might want to create a new one for this project, as your 20 similar photos of a couple of random household objects are probably not very interesting to share!)

The most important thing is to upload your photos somewhere they can be accessed without a login so that your ML system can access them and learn from them.

TRAIN YOUR MODEL

1. Go to *https://machinelearningforkids.co.uk/*. Create a new ML project, name it **Confuse the computer**, and set it to learn to recognize images.

NOTE   *If you're not sure how to create an ML project, read the section "Creating a New ML Project" on page 9 in Chapter 2.*

2. Click **Train**, as shown in Figure 14-3.

Figure 14-3: Click **Train** to prepare your training buckets.

3. Click **Add new label** and create two training buckets, as shown in Figure 14-4. Name them after the two objects that you have chosen. (The name you choose won't have any effect on the training, but it's useful for you.) I named mine grapefruit and lemon.

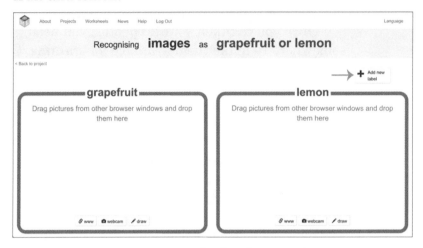

Figure 14-4: Prepare two training buckets for your objects.

4. Add the training images to your training buckets. To do so, arrange two browser windows side by side, as shown in Figure 14-5. One should have your training buckets, and the other should have the photo sharing website with your photographs.

Drag the images from the photo sharing site and drop them into the appropriate training bucket.

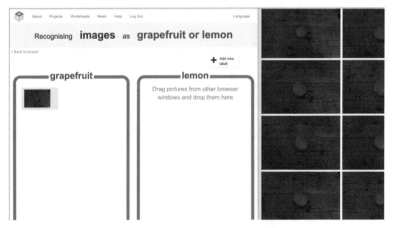

Figure 14-5: Arrange two browser windows side by side and drag the photos into your training buckets.

5. Repeat step 4 until you've got all 20 photos in your training buckets, as shown in Figure 14-6.

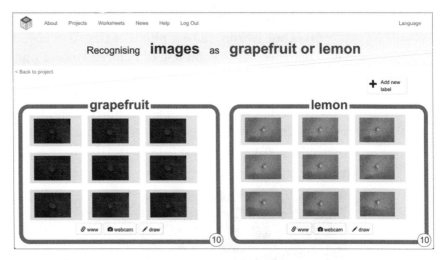

Figure 14-6: Drag all of your photos into the training buckets.

6. Click **Back to project** in the top-left corner of the screen.
7. Click **Learn & Test**.
8. Click **Train new machine learning model**, as shown in Figure 14-7.

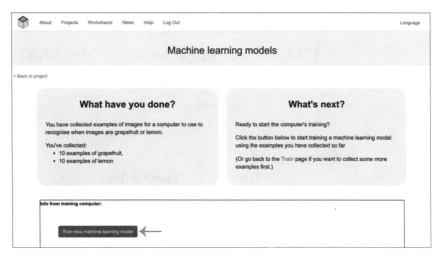

Figure 14-7: Start training an ML model.

It will take a few minutes for your ML model to train. While you're waiting, continue to the next step to prepare your project.

PREPARE YOUR PROJECT

Take another photograph of each of your two objects, *but this time, switch the backgrounds.*

In other words, take a photo of the first object where you took the photos of the second object before. Take a photo of the second object where you took the photos of the first object before.

For me, that meant taking a photo of the lemon on a dark wooden floor, and a photo of the grapefruit on a brightly lit cream carpet. Compare the test photos I took in Figure 14-8 with the training photos in Figures 14-1 and 14-2.

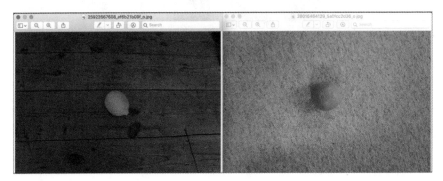

Figure 14-8: Swap the backgrounds for your test photos.

You don't need to upload these photos anywhere. You just need access to them on your computer to be able to use them for testing.

1. Click **Back to project** and then click **Make**, as shown in Figure 14-9.

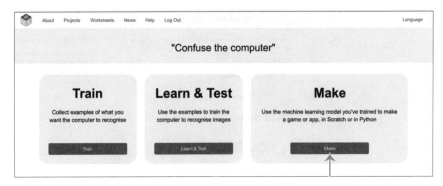

Figure 14-9: Time to make your test!

2. Click **Scratch 3**, as shown in Figure 14-10.

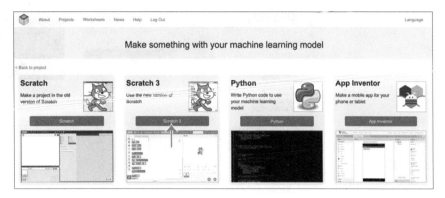

*Figure 14-10: Click **Scratch 3** to test your model.*

3. Click **Open in Scratch 3**.

4. Move your mouse pointer over the Choose a Sprite icon (the cat face) in the bottom-right corner. Click **Upload Sprite** as shown in Figure 14-11. Upload one of your two new test photos.

Figure 14-11: Upload a new sprite.

5. Copy the script shown in Figure 14-12. This script tries to recognize the sprite costume image and displays what your ML model recognizes the photo as.

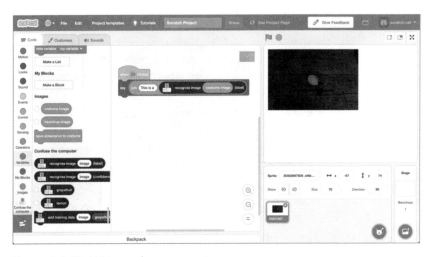

Figure 14-12: Write a short test script.

6. Click **Upload Sprite** again to upload your second test photograph. Create the same script as before for your second sprite, as shown in Figure 14-13.

Figure 14-13: Upload a second sprite and add another test script.

TEST YOUR PROJECT

It's time to run your test! Your scripts should classify both of your new test photos and display what your ML model recognized them as. Click the Green Flag to test your ML model.

My results are shown in Figure 14-14.

As you may have expected, your ML model probably gave the wrong answer.

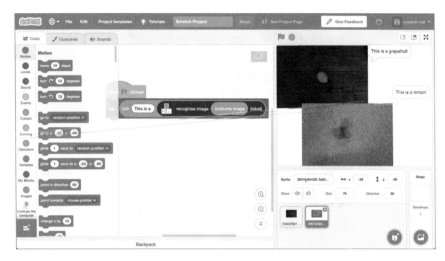

Figure 14-14: Test results for my ML model

I trained an ML model with state-of-the-art advanced technology, but it couldn't tell the difference between a lemon and a grapefruit—something that a person can do easily.

Why do you think it went so wrong?

REVIEW AND FIX YOUR PROJECT

There are several reasons why my ML model gave the wrong answer.

Think about the area taken up in the photos. The object made up about 5 percent of the overall area of my photos. About 95 percent of each photo was the background, as shown in Figure 14-15.

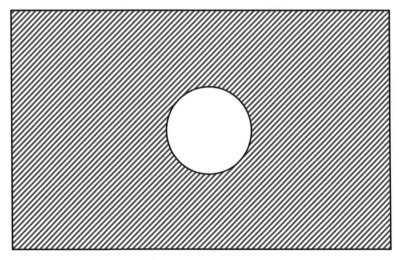

Figure 14-15: Most of my photos were background.

When you collect training examples to create an ML model, you're asking the computer to identify what those examples have in common so that it can recognize when it's given something with similar characteristics in the future.

When I tested my model with the photo of a lemon, 95 percent of the photo was very, very similar to 95 percent of all of the training photos of grapefruits in Figure 14-1. There was nothing in the way that we trained the ML model to make it clear that the part we were interested in was just that 5 percent of the photo in the middle, not the rest.

When you look at the training photos and the test photos side by side, you can see why the model made the choice it did.

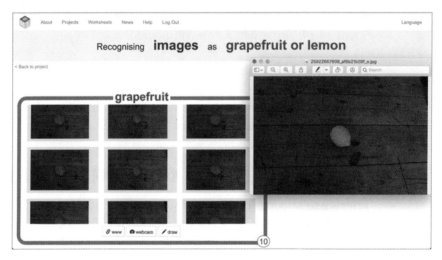

Figure 14-16: Compare the test and training photos to understand why the ML model was wrong.

Taking the photos as a whole, the largest part of my test photo (on the right of Figure 14-16) is very similar to the largest part of every training photo I had labeled as "grapefruit."

ML systems are designed to identify and recognize patterns in the examples you give them—but *these won't necessarily be the patterns that you intended or that you would've recognized.*

Can you think of a way to fix your project?

There are several things you could do. For example, if your object made up a much more significant proportion of the overall image, as shown in Figure 14-17, that might help.

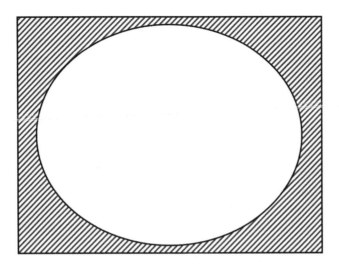

Figure 14-17: Try making your object larger in the photos.

But this solution would be useful only for projects where you could be sure that all test images would show a similarly large object.

The only thing your training examples should have in common are the attributes that you want the ML model to recognize.

For this project, the best way to be sure of that is to take lots of photos of your two objects with different places, backgrounds, lighting, sizes, angles, and orientations. Change everything that you can think of between the training examples, so that the only thing they have in common is the object itself.

For example, Figure 14-18 shows a much better set of training images for my grapefruit.

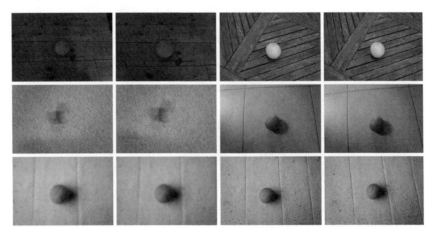

Figure 14-18: A better way to train the ML model

Varying the training images' backgrounds, lighting, and level of focus is a good start toward training the ML model to identify only the grapefruit itself as the common factor among the images.

We could make the training even better still. For example, these training images all have the grapefruit in the same position and at the same size. That's fine if I can guarantee that objects in my test photos will be at the same size and position when I test the model. But for a truly flexible model, I could also add photos where the grapefruit is at different sizes and positions.

Try improving your training examples for your two objects and training a new ML model.

If you vary the training examples, does the model pass your test?

WHAT YOU LEARNED

In this chapter, you've learned how important it is to have variation in your training sets. Whether it's a military project that accidentally recognizes the weather instead of camouflaged tanks, a university research project inventing a ruler detector instead of a skin cancer classifier, or simply a system that can't tell a grapefruit from a lemon, you've seen the impact of having *unintentional bias* in the datasets used to train an ML model.

In the next chapter, you'll see the risks of introducing *intentional bias* in ML projects.

15
BIASING THE COMPUTER

n the last chapter, you saw how it's possible to accidentally train an ML system in a way that causes it to give the wrong answer, by introducing *bias* into your training examples.

In this chapter, you'll see how bias is sometimes introduced intentionally to influence the answers that an ML system gives. You'll create an app that recommends movies to people based on the sort of films that they like. But you'll train your model in a way that lets you affect the recommendations.

BUILD YOUR PROJECT

Choose three movies to begin building the movie library that your recommendation app will have to choose from.

I want my recommendation app to help people find classic movies, so I chose three films from the 1920s, as shown in Figure 15-1, but you can choose newer movies for your project.

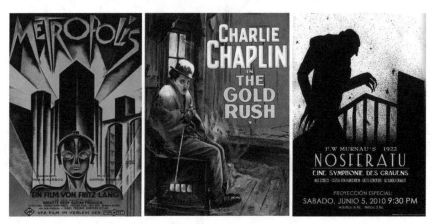

Figure 15-1: The movies I chose to start my project

Choose three very different films that different sorts of people might enjoy.

I chose the science-fiction film *Metropolis*, the comedy movie *The Gold Rush*, and the horror film *Nosferatu*.

TRAIN YOUR MODEL

1. Go to *https://machinelearningforkids.co.uk/*. Create a new ML project, name it **Bias**, and set it to learn to recognize text in your preferred language.

NOTE *If you're not sure how to create an ML project, read the section "Creating a New ML Project" on page 9 in Chapter 2.*

2. Click **Train**, as shown in Figure 15-2.

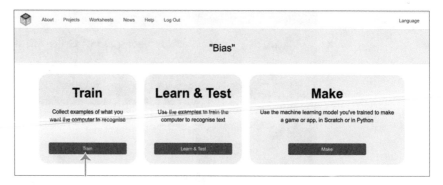

Figure 15-2: Train is the first phase of an ML project.

3. Click **Add new label**, as shown in Figure 15-3, to add a training bucket for each of your three movies.

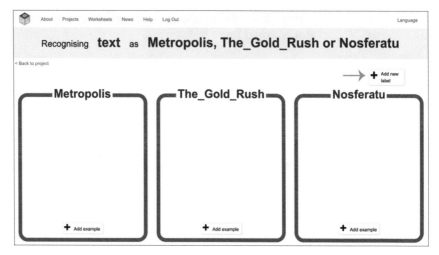

Figure 15-3: Create a training bucket for each movie.

4. Click **Add example**, as shown in Figure 15-4, in the first of your movie training buckets. Type something that you think someone who would like your first movie might say.

For example, my first movie, *Metropolis*, is a sci-fi film set in the future, so I typed **I love futuristic films**.

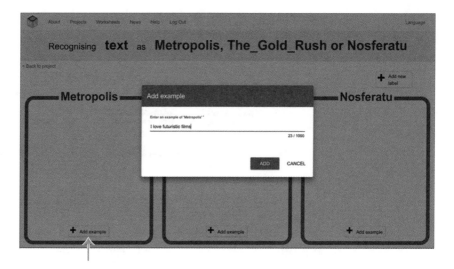

Figure 15-4: Add an example of something someone who likes the first movie would say.

5. Click **Add**.

6. Repeat steps 4 and 5 until you've got five examples of statements for each movie, as shown in Figure 15-5.

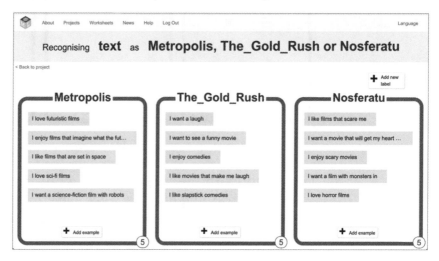

Figure 15-5: Add five examples for each movie.

7. Click **Back to project** in the top-left corner of the screen.

8. Click **Learn & Test**.

9. Click **Train new machine learning model**, as shown in Figure 15-6.

It will take a minute for the computer to learn from your examples and create a new ML model, but you can continue to the next step while you're waiting.

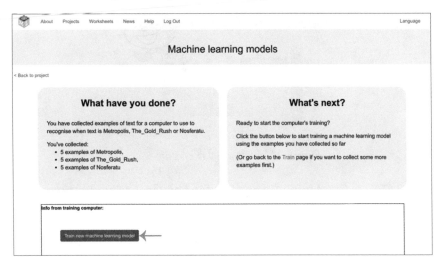

Figure 15-6: Create an ML model.

PREPARE YOUR PROJECT

Now that you have an ML model, it's time to create the recommendations app that will use it.

1. Click **Back to project** in the top-left corner of the screen.
2. Click **Make**.
3. Click **Scratch 3**, and then click **Open in Scratch 3** to open a new window with Scratch.
4. Click the **Costumes** tab, move your mouse pointer over the Choose a Costume icon (the cat face) at the bottom left, and then click **Upload Costume** to upload a poster of your movie, as shown in Figure 15-7.

NOTE *To review how to save pictures from the internet to your computer, see step 1 on page 56 in Chapter 5. If you haven't saved a picture of the movie poster to your computer, you can instead click **Paint** in the Choose a Costume menu to draw your own poster or write the movie title.*

Figure 15-7: Upload a costume.

5. Upload a poster for the first of your movies, as shown in Figure 15-8.

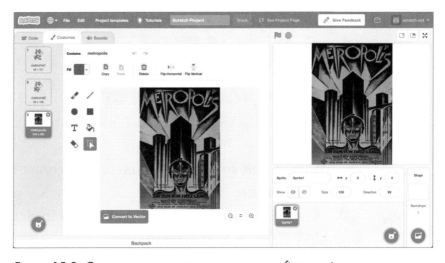

Figure 15-8: Create a costume to represent your first movie.

6. Repeat steps 4 and 5 to add the posters for all three of your movies as costumes *for the same sprite* so that it looks like Figure 15-9.

    Name each costume to match its film title.

NOTE   *Make sure you don't add the posters as separate sprites. If you've added them correctly—as three costumes for one sprite—your screen will look like Figure 15-9.*

Figure 15-9: Create a costume for each movie.

7. Click the **Code** tab and copy the script shown in Figure 15-10. You'll need to update it to use the names of your three movies.

This script will ask someone what sort of movies they like and then use your ML model to make a recommendation from the three movies in your library.

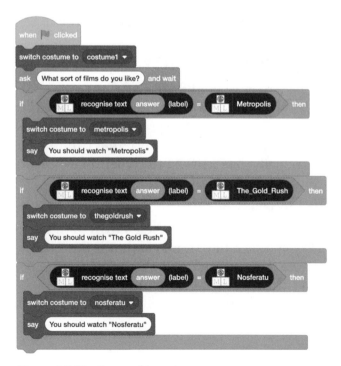

Figure 15-10: Create this script.

8. Design your project to look how you think a movie recommendation app should look. You can use the paint editor (Chapter 3), take photos with a webcam (Chapter 4), upload a picture you've saved to the computer (Chapter 5), or choose a premade design from the Scratch libraries (Chapter 5) to update the backdrop and sprite. Be creative! Figure 15-11 shows my app.

Figure 15-11: Design your movie recommendation app.

9. Click **File ▶ Save to your computer** to save your project.

TEST YOUR PROJECT

Click the Green Flag and test your project.

Try typing a variety of sentences that describe the movies that you enjoy and see what your project recommends. Avoid using words or phrases that you put in the original training buckets to see if your ML model has learned to recognize new sentences.

INTRODUCE BIAS

Click **Back to project** and then **Train** to return to the Train phase.

Now choose a fourth movie that is a bit similar to one of your first three. For my project, I chose *Frankenstein*, a horror film that's a little similar to *Nosferatu*.

Click **Add new label** to add a new training bucket for your fourth film.

Delete a few of the training examples from the first film (*Nosferatu* in my case) and add them to your new film (*Frankenstein* for me) instead.

You should end up with something like Figure 15-12.

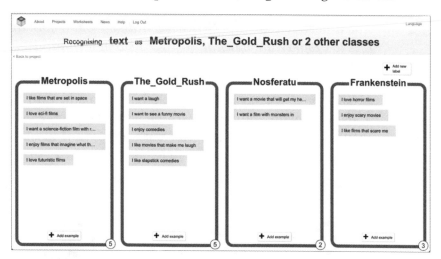

Figure 15-12: Move a few of the examples to the new film.

Add another 12 examples to your new movie. You should end up with something like Figure 15-13.

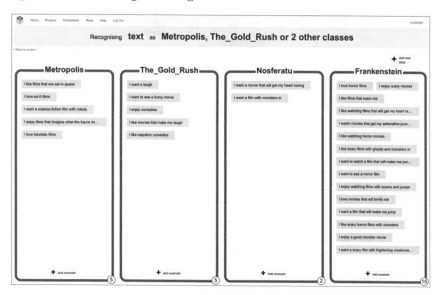

Figure 15-13: Training examples for the new movie

Click **Back to project** and then **Learn & Test**. Train a new ML model with the updated training examples.

When the training is finished, click **Back to project** and **Make** and then open **Scratch 3** again.

NOTE *You'll need to close the Scratch window from before and open a new one to display the block with your new movie name.*

Click **File ▶ Load from your computer** to open the Scratch project that you saved before. Update it to add your new movie. This will mean adding a costume with the poster for your new movie and updating the script with a fourth **if** block to recognize and recommend your new movie, as shown in Figure 15-14.

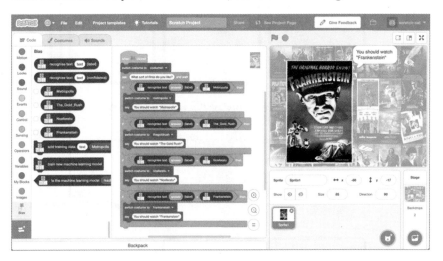

Figure 15-14: Update your project to add the fourth movie.

TEST YOUR BIASED PROJECT

Try testing your project again. You should find that it has a preference for the new fourth movie, particularly over the one that's similar to it.

For my project, that means if I mention anything about scary films, getting my heart racing or my adrenaline pumping, or monsters, my ML model will always recommend *Frankenstein* now—not *Nosferatu* as it did before. It isn't balanced between sometimes recommending one and sometimes the other. It seems to have a preference, or a bias, toward *Frankenstein*. In fact, it's difficult to get it to recommend *Nosferatu* at all unless I type a sentence exactly like one of my training examples.

Experiment with your project to see how it performs. Every ML model behaves a little differently, so try to get a feel for how the one you've trained is working.

REVIEW YOUR PROJECT

We talked in Chapter 8 about ways to measure the performance of an ML model, such as *precision* and *recall*. If you calculate some of these values before and after you intentionally bias your ML model, you can measure how bias impacts your project.

When you think you've identified the way your ML model is behaving, the next step is to understand why. Look at Figure 15-13 again. Why is my ML model recommending *Frankenstein* more often?

When you collect training examples, you're asking the computer to identify patterns in those examples, which it uses to learn to recognize new samples in the future. The number of examples you put in each bucket is one area where the computer looks for patterns. By putting many more examples in the *Frankenstein* training bucket, I influenced the ML model in a way that went beyond the individual training examples.

Say you're teaching a child to recommend movies. Imagine you tell them 5 times that they should recommend Movie A, and 1,000 times you tell them that they should recommend Movie B. What impact would that have on their expectations? If you tell them over and over again that the right answer is Movie B, they'll probably learn that the movie they should recommend is almost always Movie B.

This is similar to the way ML systems behave. The computer looks for patterns in all of your training examples in many, many ways. Your training tells it which of those ways it should trust more than others. If the training examples tell it over and over again that the patterns, techniques, and processes that tend to result in the answer Movie B are correct, it learns to trust those patterns, techniques, and processes. If the training examples tell it over and over again that the patterns, techniques, and processes that result in the answer Movie A are wrong, it learns not to trust them.

Even if it identifies patterns, techniques, and processes that result in the answer Movie A in the future, your training examples have trained it not to trust them and to prefer instead those that suggest Movie B.

As you have seen, the amount of training data in each bucket is an important factor in creating ML systems. An imbalance in the number of training examples in the different buckets can result in what we call a *biased* system.

THE CASE FOR BIAS

In most of the projects in this book so far, we've tried to keep the number of training examples in each bucket roughly the same. This is a common principle in many ML projects in an attempt to minimize bias.

But while bias is an important factor to keep in mind, it's not necessarily always a bad thing.

Say you're training a computer to recognize the difference between three possible outcomes: X, Y, and Z. Imagine that X and Y are very common; they are almost always the right answer. Outcome Z is possible, but it's very, very rare. Even though Z hardly ever happens, you want to train the computer to be able to recognize it when it does.

A balanced set of training examples, with the same number of examples for X, Y, and Z, might not be appropriate here. Having more training examples for X and Y, and fewer for Z, might train the ML model that X and Y are more likely, and in this case that's correct. Outcomes X and Y *are* more common, and Z is rare. Such a system would still be biased, but the bias reflects the statistical likelihood of the different outcomes, and so it might actually be appropriate and helpful.

AI AND ETHICS

Throughout this chapter, we've seen that the training you provide to an ML system will strongly influence the answers that it gives. What do you think this means for the responsibilities of the people who create AI systems? Do you think AI developers have an ethical responsibility to balance their training data or to avoid creating biased systems?

Does intention make a difference? If someone accidentally develops a biased system, is this more or less ethical than someone who wanted to influence the output of their system and intentionally skewed their training data?

Does money make a difference? In other words, if the producer of my fourth movie paid me lots of money to make my movie recommendation app prefer their movie over their competitors' movies, would this be more or less ethical than me making a biased app that wouldn't personally benefit me?

Does the subject make a difference? In other words, do you think that a biased AI movie recommendation app is less of an ethical concern than an AI app that makes medical treatment recommendations to doctors?

Imagine an ML recommendation app that recommends which medicines should be prescribed to patients. Each training bucket is a type of medicine, and the training examples it contains are medical records of patients for whom that medicine was the best treatment. Systems like this are in use today. ML systems can learn to recognize patterns in massive numbers of detailed medical records and combine this with evidence extracted from equally massive amounts of medical research and literature. It's still early days for this sort of medical AI assistant application, but usage is going to increase significantly in the next few years.

Now that you've seen for yourself how easy it is for such a system to be influenced to prefer one answer over another, does this affect your opinion of how such systems are used? In theory, it's possible that the manufacturer of one drug could reward the developers of a medical AI application for biasing their ML model to prefer that drug over drugs from other manufacturers.

We are increasingly relying on ML systems to make important decisions that affect people's lives. It's not just in healthcare, either. ML systems make financial recommendations that banks and loan companies use to determine whether someone should be offered insurance, whether they can get a loan, or what interest rate they should be charged. ML systems will soon be driving the cars and trucks on our roads. And there are many more examples.

Forcing companies to be transparent and disclose how their ML systems are trained might be one way to protect against ethical problems. But you've seen how much effort is involved in preparing training data. Companies invest a lot of time and money in the training data they collect to make their ML systems better than those of their competitors, so many prefer to keep their training data secret. How would you balance these ethics issues with the commercial interests of companies?

Do you think protections are needed over how AI systems are trained or applied? If so, should AI ethics policies be developed by individual companies or by the government?

This chapter is ending with more questions than answers, and this reflects the current state of ethics in AI. ML systems have the potential to improve all of our lives by training computers to do things that we couldn't do otherwise. However, as a society, we need to address a number of questions about how comfortable we are applying this technology.

WHAT YOU LEARNED

In this final project, you built on your knowledge of bias from Chapter 14 and created an ML model for a movie recommendation app that preferred one result over the others. You saw that having an imbalance in the number of examples used to train an ML model is another way to intentionally introduce bias into a system. You also learned that bias isn't necessarily bad—and in some cases may even be appropriate—but it's important to be aware of the ethical issues surrounding it, especially as AI systems become more common.

AFTERWORD

For a lot of people, AI brings to mind visions of robots and science fiction. Hopefully you've learned from the projects in this book that AI is already here, and it is all around us.

Understanding how ML systems are created gives you a better understanding of how the world around you works. That understanding provides insight into how companies know what you're thinking and recommend products you might like. And it helps you recognize that when you're asked to rate something, or prove you're a human, or tag a face in a photo, you're probably training someone's ML system.

THE FUTURE

If our lives are all going to be impacted by ML systems in the future, we might have an opinion on how they are trained and applied.

For example, what applications are appropriate for ML systems, and what decisions should be left to humans?

Should machines make decisions involving your healthcare? Or how law enforcement behaves? Or who can get a credit card or a mortgage?

Who should be responsible for collecting the training data used to create the most important ML systems? And who should be checking how training is done? How should ML systems be tested, and should you be able to see the results of those tests for the ML systems you use?

The fundamentals that you've learned in this book—such as the impact of the amount and balance of training data on ML models, the measures we use to describe an ML model's performance, and the sorts of things that can go wrong—are all useful to get you thinking about these important questions.

They're also an essential starting point if you choose to study ML further and learn about how different ML systems are implemented. I hope that this book has encouraged you to explore more.

NEXT STEPS

If you'd like to learn more, one option is to build your own ML project. Many of the AI projects created by companies around the world are built using online ML services provided "in the cloud," just as you've been doing so far. With these services, you provide the training data, the cloud service creates an ML model using it, and then you test the model to make sure it does the job that you need. You can continue using Scratch if you want, or progress to using a text-based programming language like Python.

Alternatively, if you'd like to understand more about how ML works, you can switch from using ML models that are built and hosted on the cloud to building and running your own ML models. This gives you more control over the behavior of your ML systems and also helps you learn how they work internally. You'll need to start using a text-based programming language, such as Python, but if you're willing to do that, there's a wide variety of free ML technology frameworks available to get you started. TensorFlow is one of the most widely used, and there are free tutorials on the TensorFlow website (*https://www.tensorflow.org/*) that will help you build your first ML model.

I hope that this book is only the start of your ML journey. Whether you use what you've learned about ML to create your own AI projects and applications, to build ML models yourself, or to understand a little more about how the online services you use every day work, I wish you luck with your next steps.

INDEX

M

Machine Educable Noughts and
    Crosses Engine
    (MENACE), 204
Machine Learning for Kids
    creating an account, 14
    creating a project, 9
    Learn & Test phase, 12
    Make phase, 13
    training buckets, 11, 47
    Train phase, 11
    Try it now, 9
machine learning (ML), xix
    definition of, 3
    ethical considerations for,
        182, 252
    fields where used, 20, 68, 82,
        148, 174, 225, 249, 252
    future of, 252
    importance of testing, 73, 93
    pattern recognition, 20, 33, 46,
        50, 84, 93, 104, 225, 234, 247
    real-world applications, 20, 68,
        82, 84, 145, 151, 182, 185,
        225, 237, 249, 252
    relationship with AI, 4
Make me happy (project), 90
    improving, 96
    preparing, 85
    testing, 96
    training, 90
making a list, 112, 115, 179
making a variable, 60, 115
MENACE (Machine Educable
    Noughts and Crosses
    Engine), 204
Michie, Donald, 204, 221
mistakes, 33, 46, 117, 128, 225
    bias, 224, 236, 246
    learning from, 99
    user feedback on, 99, 178
ML. *See* machine learning (ML)
Ms. Pac-Man competition, 186

N

natural language, definition of, 152
natural language interface, 152, 165

negative training examples, 133
neural networks, 4, 202, 204
Newspapers (project), 106
    improving, 118
    preparing, 110
    testing, 114, 117
    training, 106

O

optical character recognition (OCR),
    67, 82

P

patterns, recognizing, 20, 33, 46, 50,
    84, 93, 104, 225, 234, 247
phases of an ML project, 11
pictures, saving from the internet,
    26, 241
playing games to evaluate ML
    models, 220
precision, 126, 143, 145, 247
project list, 9, 16
projects
    Animal sorter, 21
    Avoid the monster, 187
    Bias, 238
    Chatbot, 169
    Confuse the computer, 225
    Find the duck, 132
    Judge a book by its cover, 52
    Make me happy, 90
    Newspapers, 106
    Rock Paper Scissors, 38
    Smart classroom, 153
    Sorting office, 69
    Tic Tac Toe, 205
project templates, xxi, 43, 75, 135,
    153, 160, 187, 205

Q

question answering (QA) systems, 168

R

real-world applications for image
    recognition systems, 145
    CAPTCHA, 146
    drones, 148
    satellite imagery, 148